Rise Up & Thrive

How to Break Cycles of Toxic and Traumatic Relationships to Create Healthy Love

Kristina Hudson, MSOT, OTR

Never underestimate your ability to RISE
Kristina Hudson

Rise Up & Thrive

How to Break Cycles of Toxic and Traumatic Relationships to Create Healthy Love

Kristina Hudson, MSOT, OTR

Copyright © 2023 - Reflek Publishing

All Rights Reserved.

For more information: hello@riseupthriving.com

Paperback ISBN: 978-1-962280-03-7
Ebook ISBN: 978-1-962280-02-0

A GIFT FOR YOU

Before we get started, grab your FREE Rise Up & Thrive Workbook as a special gift from me. The workbook has more than 50 pages to help you integrate the teachings as you go, including:

- A Life Audit Worksheet
- A 30-day Self Care Bingo Card
- A THRIVEMAPP Worksheet
- Journal Prompts
- Favorite Resources List

To grab it for free, visit www.risewithkristina.com/book1 or snap the QR code below.

Dedication

This book is dedicated to my grandmother, Tutu, who inspired me, supported me, and guided me in the physical world and beyond.

Table Of Contents

Epigraph

9/13/2019
This is your rising
Your rising from the ashes
From the darkest depths
From the unknown and the uncertainty
From sheer terror
From your own demons
When everything is stripped away from you
You only have two choices
You can either stand on your own two feet
Or you can allow the ash to consume you
In this moment you know
You spread your beautiful wings
You acknowledge that you have the power to create your destiny
And you become the whole damn rising
This is your rebirth

Introduction

2019

In therapy, as I was peeling the layers back, I was seeing things for what they truly were for the first time. I realized the level of toxicity that existed in my marriage. I began to hear others say that what I experienced was abuse, though I was having a hard time wrapping my head around it. And I was starting to learn that this experience didn't birth itself from nothing, but rather had roots deep in my childhood and life experiences.

Over the next several years, I would begin to realize that if I did not want to put myself through that again, I needed to work on healing old wounds. I needed to take care of myself in a way I had not been cared for in the past. I needed to see myself not as broken but rather as a person who had experienced a lot of pain, hurt and trauma.

I had to learn who I was and who I wanted to become. I needed to believe that I was worthy of love, respect, compassion, and happiness. I had to understand that no one was coming to rescue me from this life and it was time for me to take my power back and save myself.

Through my self-reflection, I began recognizing patterns in my healing process as well as those around me. From that I created the R.I.S.E. Method, which is a powerful framework designed to support you in your recovery and healing journey after traumatic, toxic, and potentially abusive relationship(s). This method consists of four essential steps: Recognition, Information Gathering, Self-Discovery, and Embodiment.

Recognition is the first step, where you begin to acknowledge and recognize the patterns, habits, and behaviors that have been present in your life. In this step, you are becoming more consciously aware of the way you are living vs. the way you want to live your life. It involves developing an awareness that things need to change for your well-being and growth. Questions, confusion, and grief may come up as you begin to recognize your past for what it was. For very rarely are your stuck points related to current life experiences. More often than not, they have roots that tie back to your early years. Recognizing the impact of past experiences and understanding the need for healing sets the stage for the transformative journey ahead.

Information Gathering involves actively seeking knowledge and understanding about why you are the way they are and why you engage in certain behaviors. The more you ask yourself, "Why?" the more you will seek answers. This phase often includes researching topics such as trauma, abuse, psychology, and personal development. By gathering information, you will gain insights into the underlying factors that have shaped your experiences, allowing you to develop a deeper understanding of yourself and your journey.

Self-Discovery is an eye-opening phase in the healing process that entails delving into the deeper layers of one's being, exploring emotions, beliefs, values, and desires. Self-discovery involves various practices such as therapy, journaling, meditation, and self-reflection. Through these practices, you will cultivate self-awareness, uncover your authentic self, and discover your own strengths, passions, and purpose.

Finally, Embodiment is the culmination of the R.I.S.E. Method. It involves embodying newfound knowledge, self-awareness, and personal growth in everyday life. It means integrating the insights and lessons learned into your thoughts, actions, and choices. Embodiment is about living authentically and aligning your life with your values, desires, and aspirations. This phase empowers you to step into your true self, embracing self-love, self-compassion, and self-empowerment.

Healing is necessary. Twice in my life, I have been forced to face my shadows that were born from unhealthy dynamics at home. I remember the first time my therapist told me, "Life is about to get really good for you. Once you are on your own, in college, you will begin to see things change for the better." That was the home life I didn't have a choice in. I was born into it. The second may have been more difficult because I chose that home life, and yet I ended up choosing something just as destructive as that which I had previously escaped.

When we don't heal past traumas, we repeat cycles. While I can't change the past, I have learned that lesson now. I know that if I had properly healed my childhood wounds, I would not have walked into a marriage that was just as destructive. In the past two years, I have done intensive therapy to work on myself. And I continue to do introspective self-healing. If you want to break the pattern, you have to be willing to do the work. It isn't easy. Most times it is really fucking difficult and messy, but I promise you it will be worth it.

The R.I.S.E. Method will provide you with a structured framework to navigate your healing and recovery process. It empowers you to recognize the need for change, gather knowledge and understanding, embark on a journey of self-discovery, and ultimately embody your newfound wisdom.

In the chapters that follow, I will guide you through this method, as well as the other strategies I utilized in my own healing journey. I share journal entries from as far back as 2003, but specifically focus on the past six years, beginning with the end of my marriage. I share my own experiences to help give you insight into the truth of what occurs behind closed doors. I also share a WINK (What I Now Know) at the end of each chapter to share from the perspective I have today.

The goal of this book is to help you identify unhealthy relationship behaviors and then to provide you with the information and strategies I used to heal so that you can create a life that you love.

WINK

Had I known then what I know now, I would have sought the right therapist, guides, and coaches when I first moved away to college. I thought that simply leaving the house was enough. I thought that was my chance to break free and leave the past behind.

Little did I know how much my past would infiltrate all of my future relationships, the beliefs I had about myself, the willingness to stand up for myself, the ability to know who I was and more. Had I known then what I know now, I would have done the healing work before entering a relationship.

Chapter 1
The Search for Happiness

2016

I feel wrong saying this out loud, but I feel so unhappy. I am grasping at straws trying to make sense of it all, trying to figure out what is wrong with me. I feel like I am tilting on an axis and I just need to get back to a place of equilibrium. I have done so much, accomplished so much and have so much – I shouldn't feel this way. When others look at my life, they don't understand why I am so miserable. Hell, I don't know why I am so miserable. I want answers and I need to feel better quickly. I feel like everything looks amazing on the outside, but this inner turmoil is eating me alive. It is literally sucking the life out of me.

"Stop looking for happiness in the same place you lost it." - Unknown

The depression was coming in waves. The feelings of unhappiness and dissatisfaction mixed with confusion and chaos. I was in the middle of creating a dream life, my dream life. The head of the VA had recently honored me for my innovative work with our Nation's Veterans. I was traveling to receive certifications, give presentations and participate in fitness competitions. From the outside looking in, I imagine it looked like I had a life that many only dream about.

I had just landed in New Jersey and looked like a kid in a candy shop, my eyes filled with wonder and my heart beat with anticipation. I was preparing for one of the biggest competitions for National Physique

Committee (NPC) bikini, but first, I desperately wanted to explore New York City. The city that was center stage to so many of the movies that influenced my younger years, to seeing the brownstones, FAO Schwarz, the Empire State Building and Broadway. It was also the city that my cousin had loved and I longed to feel connected to him once more. I was due for some exercise, so I donned my running shoes and caught the next bus.

The next morning I woke up after a restless night, grateful to have a makeup artist who would hide the sleepiness on my face. I usually loved the glam that came with makeup, the sparkling bikini and my deep bronze tan. Today, though, I felt like I had been on a constant chase but could no longer remember if I was running toward or away from something.

I held onto the rickety metal railing as I stepped up the stairs, not trusting my clear plastic heels to hold me up. I knew I looked the part, but I could not even bring myself to smile. I loved being under the lights of the stage; I loved being able to perform the routine I had practiced hours on end until I found myself dreaming through each step, but today, all I could think about was the juicy hamburger I would indulge in later that evening.

As I pressured my friends to stuff our faces with candy between preliminaries and finals, I kept finding myself thinking, "I don't even care about this shit. Why am I here? Why did I just spend thousands of dollars to fly across the country when all I want right now is a big fat burger?"

Even after returning home, I ruminated on the same questions. I started asking, "What am I even doing? And why am I doing these things if they aren't making me happy?"

I would not have accepted the diagnosis of depression at the time. I would have simply said my life was out of balance and insisted that I needed to find my homeostasis. I needed to create a balance in my life so that I could be happy (again). I googled things like, "How to be happy?" I immediately dove off the deep end into anything and everything that could fix my situation; that could fix me.

I discovered my initial teachers of personal development, including Oprah, Tony Robbins, and Deepak Chopra. I committed to regular meditation anytime Oprah and Deepak launched their quarterly challenges. I watched YouTube videos and read every article I could find, anything that could teach me how to be happy.

I first discovered the power of mindset work and the ability to create the life that we deserve. I began focusing on the various areas of my life and evaluating what needed to change.

This may have been my first taste of truly believing in self-love, self-care, and self-worth. A few months later, I began to truly question my marriage and started contemplating divorce. While I would not have admitted that my marriage was the source of my unhappiness, I began uncovering the many components that led me to feel the way I did.

I was beginning to better understand what I could bring to the table and what was lacking in return. I was tired of over-giving and over-doing, with little reciprocation in return. I was tired of feeling like I wasn't enough and begging for my husband to show me affection.

I finally put my foot down on what may have been my first boundary. I informed my husband that I would no longer be funding our vacations. If traveling was important to him, he needed to contribute as well.

I don't recall there being fear with this assertiveness because, for the first time, I didn't care what the response was. Something would change or it wouldn't, and this time, if he didn't take responsibility, I was okay with staying home.

I believe that my newfound confidence came from two places. First, in the past two and a half years, I had invested heavily in myself and my fitness competitions, to the point where I continued to prove to myself how strong I was and how much [will]power I truly had. I also proved that I could connect with others beyond the walls of my marriage and find people who were truly interested in being in my life. Second, when taking the initiative to explore my own development, I was showing myself what I could do with these recently realized superpowers.

There were many reasons I lacked confidence and found myself in a relationship where I was not valued, nor was I appreciated. Looking back, I know it wasn't the effect of one or two incidents, but rather chronic behavior patterns that resulted in the stories I had adopted and believed to be true.

WINK

In the beginning, I believe I had a hard time naming the root of my unhappiness, in part because I wasn't willing to see it and maybe because inadequate life balance was a socially acceptable reason. Much of the research I was doing also alluded to the idea that overworking equals dissatisfaction, and I felt more than overworked. I was working in the typical way in my career, excessively working around the clock in the gym to be show ready, and working hard to do whatever I could to make my marriage something, or anything, better than it was.

But what made me stay so long? What made me put in so much effort when I wasn't getting anything in return? These were some questions I continued to ask myself. It wasn't until years later that I began to understand the need to get to the root of the problem. For far too long, I thought that if I just pushed it down or pushed it aside, I could keep pretending that things were good and that I was happy with the life I had accepted.

The day that I admitted to myself that I refused to do this again was the day I was determined to not only find the root, but to do everything I could to get it out.

Activity

Before I even realized what I was doing, or the long-term implications, I decided to conduct a life audit. I sat down and took the time to look at the primary categories that made up my life and asked myself a variety of questions. Just as we take time to audit our finances or work performance, it is important to audit our lives on a regular basis. This will give you the information you may need about your levels of satisfaction, what is going well, what isn't, and what might need to change. A life audit is an intentional evaluation of each area of your life so that you can move in the direction of your dreams.

You can find a life audit exercise at www.risewithkristina.com/book1

Chapter 2
Toxic Relationship Cycles

10/9/2019

Two years ago, I filed for divorce. It was far from an easy decision, but once I made it, I knew there was no going back. Two things became apparent to me: first, I ignored and dismissed many red flags throughout my relationship. And second, I was unable to grasp the sheer magnitude of the abuse and manipulation until after I was out of the situation.

I learned I had deeply rooted beliefs. For example, I made a vow that I would stand by my husband no matter what. Honestly, I made excuse after excuse as to why I needed to stay. Regardless, it takes a huge amount of courage to leave a relationship of nearly fourteen years. I felt shame, embarrassment, fear, anxiety, doubt, sadness, and, at times, hopelessness. For years, I was told no one would ever love me. For years, I was belittled and torn to pieces. It is hard, even for me, to imagine how I could crumble behind closed doors, being the "strong and independent woman" that I believed myself to be.

"Trauma is not just an event that took place sometime in the past; it is also the imprint left by that experience on the mind, brain, and body." – Dr. Bessel van der Kolk

While this book focuses on the toxic relationship cycles within our intimate partnerships, it is important to also identify the influence of intergenerational trauma. Intergenerational trauma is when an adult inadvertently creates experiences for their own children which are similar to those of their own unresolved trauma. While it can be challenging to admit that you need to process your experiences, those who avoid the work may replicate those traumatic experiences whenever triggered.

Intergenerational trauma often leads us to imitate the behaviors that were modeled to us both with our intimate partner and our children. The cycle looks something like this: Your grandparents likely experienced a lot of hardships and parenting styles were quite different back then. This influenced the way your parents were raised, and the behaviors they had modeled for them. For most, acknowledging emotional needs, taking a child's opinion into consideration, and displaying compassion were non-existent. Instead, a lot of children experienced parents who were emotionally unavailable, whether that meant that they were always working and never present, or those who didn't have the capacity to understand how to connect on a deeper level with their children. Others were raised with the idea that a whip was a standard form of punishment. And unfortunately, without self-reflection and self-inquiry, parents simply acted the only way they knew how. This type of trauma looks like uninformed and unhealed individuals attempting to parent based on their own experiences, no matter how toxic, unhealthy, or potentially traumatic these behaviors may be. Whether you can reflect back on your childhood and identify things as dysfunctional, neglectful, abusive or not having your needs met, these events create a lasting impact.

One thing I feel is important to note here is that your childhood doesn't have to look a certain way to have led you to engage in toxic relationships. Often, women seek help for lack of fulfillment, dissatisfaction, or unhappiness, only to find out there are deeply rooted beliefs from childhood. My clients who are the most surprised to learn about their unhealed wounds are those who believed they had a really good childhood. Unfortunately, even when parents are acting out of love, their behaviors are not always loving or what you needed as a child.

For example, I have worked with women whose families didn't have a lot of money and therefore, their parents had multiple jobs that kept them away from the home. While this was done out of love and wanting to provide for their children, this also resulted in the child feeling neglected and alone. Children are incapable of the cognitive processing required to make sense of things with logic. Therefore, they make it mean whatever makes sense to them at the time. They may believe that they don't matter, or they may develop hyper-independent tendencies because they were always left to fend for themselves.

It wasn't until I was in therapy, after my marriage ended, that I realized I had, in fact, continued the cycle. Previously, I thought "the cycle" only referred to the way I would raise my children. With that in mind, when I was twelve years old, I declared I would never be a mom and I never wanted to have kids. I was terrified of not knowing how to raise a child, but even worse, raising my child from the hell that I knew. I had often heard that abusers were likely children of abuse, almost as a justification, but once I had heard it, I knew I would not inflict that kind of pain on another child. That cycle would end with me.

Research shows that individuals who have suffered abuse as children are significantly more likely to abuse their own kids. A study that was conducted by the Department of Health and Human Services in 2019 provides evidence of these intergenerational trauma cycles.

- It is estimated that 1/3 of adults who experienced neglect as children will go on to abuse their own children or children in their care, with even greater numbers for those who experienced physical abuse.[1]

- Nearly 3/4 of all perpetrators of child maltreatment, abuse and neglect are parents of the victim.[1]
- Mothers who experience more stress, depression, anxiety, dependency and immaturity are more likely to reenact their own maltreatment on their children.[3]
- The long-term consequences of childhood maltreatment are vast and impact physical, psychological, interpersonal, cognitive and behavioral systems.[1]

Childhood experiences of trauma, such as physical or emotional abuse, neglect, or loss, can leave deep emotional wounds. When these wounds are left unaddressed and unresolved, they can impact how individuals relate to themselves and others. Unresolved trauma can lead to difficulties with trust, emotional intimacy, and vulnerability in adult relationships. It may also contribute to defensive or self-protective behaviors that hinder healthy relationships later on.

The problem when you have experienced unhealthy or abusive relationships as a child, you don't know what a healthy relationship looks like. Once dating, you may be quick to dismiss or justify your partner's behavior because you believe you are in love, and you don't believe they meant to act in that way, or worse, you believe this is normal behavior because it resembles what you saw growing up.

Through my own healing, I also discovered that our unresolved trauma leads us to seek partners who we believe will "fix us" or heal our wounds. We are desperate to have our needs met, which often sets us up for unhealthy and potentially abusive dynamics. From the beginning, consciously or subconsciously, we look for a partner who will be our caretaker, provider, and savior.

We are often drawn to those behaviors that are familiar. Even if those behaviors, or people, are not healthy, they are what we know.

Women who experienced childhood maltreatment stay in toxic dynamics because of low self-esteem and a belief that abuse, power and control are normal in relationships. In that instance, our most basic instinct is to believe that it is safer to stay in what is known than to risk uncertainty. However, to break the cycle, you must be willing to take the leap.

I share these statistics to emphasize the reality of toxic and abusive relationship cycles. What I later learned, however, is that by doing the healing work, we can stop the toxic and abusive patterns before they are passed down to our kids.

Research has been conducted in the areas of intergenerational trauma (abuse leading to people becoming abusers) since the 1960s, with a variance of 7%-60% of those repeating the maltreatment. However, more recent studies are providing new evidence that intergenerational trauma is not inevitable.[4]

Some of the factors that the research identifies as contributors of breaking cycles include safe, stable and nurturing adult relationships; engagement with a therapist; lower levels of life and financial stress; and fewer symptoms of depression and anxiety.[4]

These findings are highly correlated to healthy and loving relationship dynamics. Therefore, recognizing these patterns, and then having the willingness to do the work to heal, is necessary to break the cycles. The cycles include both what is passed down to your children as well as the relationships you continue to engage in. When you are able to self-reflect and take responsibility for your healing, you are able to have healthy relationships.

WINK

There is a saying that hurt people hurt people, but healed people can also heal others. This is why it is so important to break the cycle and let the trauma or unhealthy relationship dynamics end with you. You may not have been able to control what happened in your past, but it is your responsibility to heal so that you can determine how you show up for your future.

Reflection

Do you know if your parents or grandparents experienced trauma? Have your parents ever discussed their own childhood and how they were raised? Take some time to consider how these patterns may have evolved and been passed down in your own family.

Chapter 3
Recognizing Toxic Patterns

7/20/2017

I don't know that you will be able to reassure me enough or make me feel safe enough to truly move forward. I feel stuck and scared. I'm scared because of the secrets you kept from me and scared because I didn't know what was really going on. I fear that it will all happen again, with time. I know I should remove the fear and let it be what it will be, but I also find myself in self-protective mode willing to do anything to protect my heart and my pride. I want someone to love me enough, want me enough and think I am worthy enough not to betray me.

7/25/2017

Despite the discussion and agreement to end private communication with women so that we can rebuild trust, it continues. How can I build trust when promises are already broken? How can I feel confident that moving forward and rebuilding our marriage is the right decision when you can't follow through on your part? If I can't trust that you will follow through on a basic scale, how can I trust that you will follow through on a larger one? I am scared to travel for work in the coming weeks, afraid of what you might do while I'm gone. I shouldn't have to feel that kind of fear and anxiety. You should be giving me reassurance not making me fall down the dark hole of mistrust, fear, hurt and sadness.

"Your willingness to look at your darkness is what empowers you to change." – Iyanla Vanzant

We arrived in Cabo San Lucas ten years after first standing on that beach and saying our vows. Our large-ish extended family eagerly agreed to this celebratory reunion. After all, ten years of marriage was a big deal, and our families were always up for a good party and an excuse to travel abroad.

From the luxurious all-inclusive resort on the beach, to the large group dinners, to the excursions, I made sure every detail would be one that we all would remember. As we walked into our suite, the bed was covered with rose petals as a beautiful sentiment for the big milestone. It was the best feeling in the world to be surrounded by those we loved and to know how much they wanted to shower us with their love and support.

I think this is where so many get it wrong. Often, when thinking about toxic or abusive relationships, I believe the perception is that it is always bad. The truth is, it is cyclical, but you never know the speed at which the cyclone will move. You never know how long you will get to hold on to the good times or have to endure the worst pain of your life.

Ten years wasn't all butterflies and rainbows, nor was it all destruction. It was the happy moments that kept me hanging on, hoping to get a glimpse of something good again, hoping to feel a sense of love once more. There were times of deep bonding, uncontrollable laughter, and showing up as a united front and unstoppable force, working together as a team. Other times, the scars would create a lifelong reminder of the suffering and pain.

There was the rare physical pain, but the cuts that hurt most were those that reinforced the old stories on replay in my mind—the betrayal reminding me that I wasn't enough, the crazy-making, and the dismissal and invalidation of my experience. I didn't realize the significance at the time; that came later with intense therapy and deep inquiry from both my therapist and me.

After what I believed was going to be a turning point for us and our relationship, things had changed, but not the way I had anticipated. It was as if, upon our return from Cabo, someone had pulled a small piece of thread, building the momentum for the unraveling that was to come.

My husband was becoming colder and more distant. The more questions I asked, the more he ridiculed me, mocked me and called me crazy. I came home one day from a work trip and noticed a faint scent of a woman's perfume that I was not familiar with. Shortly thereafter, I discovered phone records that revealed conversations lasting several hours while my husband wouldn't spend five minutes with me on the phone. When I tried to talk with him, he seemed as though he were in another universe, his attention was anywhere but with me. After being called crazy so many times, I began to wonder if maybe I was. Until the day that the seen could not remain unseen. That was the day that my world came crashing down and simultaneously the light shone on a place within me that had been dark for too long.

I am a firm believer that the longevity of a relationship should not be the determining factor of success. Too often, we suppress, ignore, and dismiss the negative aspects to keep the peace. This works until it doesn't. This works until the reality of the situation becomes too painful to ignore. And unfortunately, when we have been taught to ignore our needs, we discover that rather than the healthy and happy relationship we believed we were creating, we are instead in the midst of unhealthy, toxic and potentially abusive dynamics.

You might be wondering how to differentiate the different types of relationship dynamics, such as those that are dysfunctional, toxic and abusive. Unfortunately, the answer isn't always clear, but it is also important to understand that unhealthy traits may exist on a spectrum.

Regardless of how you define a relationship, though, they all have the potential to be traumatic.

Abusive relationships are those which are defined by one person enacting power and control over another, whereas relationships that would be defined as toxic typically look like two ill-equipped individuals bringing out the unhealed wounds in each other. That being said, both types of relationships can create lasting traumatic effects.

Relationship cycles, even toxic ones, are not usually apparent at first. Most people initially present to therapy or begin doing their "me-search" because they are unhappy or unfulfilled in their life. They feel like something is wrong with them for not being grateful for all that they have. Even when confiding in friends or family, they are often encouraged to look at the positive aspects of their life, or their feelings may be dismissed.

Some initial thoughts might sound like,

- Why am I so ungrateful, my life is pretty good. It's definitely better than most.
- My husband isn't that bad. At least he doesn't hit me.
- I don't have anyone to talk to about it. From the outside, our relationship looks perfect.
- Am I a terrible person for wanting something more?
- Is this really all there is [to life]?

Can you relate to any of these?

The truth is, there are reasons you were attracted to your partner. There are reasons you were attracted to much of the life you live today. But that doesn't mean things can't or don't change. You have grown and you may want something more. You may feel as though your partner isn't growing at the same speed or in the same direction as you. You may feel like you always thought they would change but they haven't. And you may also be in the midst of an unhealthy relationship that you once settled into for one reason or another.

This would be a good opportunity to take inventory of your relationship.

- What about it is good?
- What about it do you wish were different?
- Do you feel safe enough to have a conversation with your partner?
- What do you think his reaction might be?

Open and honest communication is always a good first step to creating healthy and happy relationships. However, these conversations must be pursued with compassionate curiosity from both parties. Most people have not been properly trained to manage their emotions or to communicate empathically. More often than not, these conversations come down to accusations and defensiveness, which is always ineffective. That being said, the way you handle these conversations doesn't automatically indicate you are in a toxic relationship. But you both should want to engage in a way that is best for both of you, individually and together.

Some signs to look for that might indicate a toxic relationship are:

- Lack of empathy and understanding
- Feeling like you can't voice your concerns
- Feeling like you have to walk on eggshells (be careful about what you say or do in the presence of your partner)

Once you have this additional insight, whether you are able to have the conversation with them or not, you can begin to take control for your part. You don't have control over your partner, but you do have control over the behavior and the relationship you are willing to tolerate.

This is also a time to reflect on the way you show up in your relationship. If you stay or if you choose to leave, how will you want to show up differently? A favorite quote of mine is, "If nothing changes, nothing changes." You have to be willing to do the introspective work to not only take responsibility for your part but to also get curious about your past conditioning that may have contributed to your current relationship.

Identifying the root cause is the way to create lasting change. Most people try to apply a "Band-Aid" to their old pain but that isn't sufficient for lifelong healing. Identifying the root also is not about placing blame but rather understanding. We must have the recognition before we can take effective action. Otherwise, you are flying in the dark, unclear of your final destination.

Again, your childhood doesn't need to be abusive to create insecure attachment, limiting beliefs or low self-esteem, all of which can negatively impact your adult relationships. But in knowing the root cause(s), you can begin to break the cycles.

You probably know by now that a perfect relationship doesn't exist. There will always be tough conversations that need to be had, challenging circumstances and the need to compromise every now and then. However, it may be difficult to know when a relationship requires too much work.

- Is there often tension in the relationship?
- Do you feel resentment toward your partner?
- Are you unhappy more than you are happy?

When you are in the midst of a relationship, it can be hard to make a blanket statement about the overall health of your dynamic. However, you may be able to identify some signs of toxicity or unhealthy relationships. If you feel a lack of support, the inability to trust your partner, or you feel a sense of resentment toward your partner, these all can be indications that your relationship is unhealthy.

WINK

Allow this book to give you permission to enter into a research phase. You don't need to take immediate action or make the decision that you need to leave your partner. Two pieces of advice that I was given, and I will pass along to you, are to make sure you are 100% sure about your decision and to have a plan.

For me, being incredibly clear and having zero doubt about my decision to walk away gave me the strength to move forward, voice my needs and not look back. I was also very methodical in the process, as you will read later, and made sure that I had my bases covered to protect myself and those around me.

Activity

Take some time to journal on the questions posed throughout this chapter. Consider whether there are themes that show up in your relationship. Take an inventory of what you like, what you don't, and what would need to change. You do not need to take immediate action, but bringing your awareness and attention to the things you can change may give you a greater sense of authority over your own life.

Chapter 4
Enough is Enough

10/11/2017

What makes me act as a caretaker? I have feelings of sadness, hurt, anger, bitterness, and disappointment. We search for partners who match our parents and seek an unfulfilled need. Caregiving makes me feel good. Maybe I'm trying to make myself feel needed, valued, and appreciated. If I can take care of myself, it will make me a better person, I will be okay, with or without him. It is time to become self-aware and mindful to heal.

3/2018

It is no wonder I married the man I did- the narcissism was comfortable and familiar. I had to work for his affection and his attention the same way I had to with her. I was regularly reminded of how she and he are superior. I was familiar with the condescending and degrading comments followed by something sweet. Someone recently said how it was odd that my mom thought of her young daughter as her caretaker. And then she implemented this all over again on the trip. Expecting me to help with her luggage, pick up the tab, look after her, etc. It was naive of me to think I could travel with her. I realized years ago I needed to distance myself from the toxicity and then I went and immersed myself right back into it. Hopefully this lesson will be learned for good now. Hopefully I can better understand how to apply this lesson to all future relationships.

"When we love ourselves enough, we stop chasing people who don't." – Vienna Pharaon

It is commonly said that we seek a partner who reminds us of our parent of the opposite sex. More recently, I heard we seek a partner who reminds us the most of the parent with whom we have unmet needs.

In my post-divorce therapy sessions, I was delving into the patterns that were being repeated in my relationships, from childhood to my intimate relationships as an adult. It finally dawned on me, for the first time, how much my ex-husband resembled my mother, or maybe more accurately, the relationship I had with my mother. It was a relationship that was anything but healthy. There were codependent, toxic, and narcissistic tendencies and occasional emotional and physical abuse. There was frequent yelling and screaming, throwing and punching. We were never taught how to manage our anger or our aggression, and we took it out on one another. I was never taught what love was supposed to look like, so I mirrored all I knew.

When I decided I was ready to date again, I was cautiously optimistic. Here I was thinking I was healing from the toxic and manipulative relationship I had just left. I started dating men who had similar behaviors to the ones I had seen before. Men who didn't value or respect me. Men who were unfaithful. Men who lied. Men who were emotionally unavailable. And more manipulation. I didn't know how deep I had to go to identify the root cause of these patterns. I was not aware of the subconscious control these old wounds and old stories had on me.

The more I recognized the patterns of my past relationship that I did not want to repeat, the more I began avoiding those who mirrored the relationship I had with my mom and instead subconsciously seeking those who would remind me of the dynamic I had with my father. However, they, too, were emotionally unavailable. I always felt the need to prove myself and to prove I was worth loving, and they always felt distant.

One day in therapy, I could finally acknowledge I was looking for someone to rescue me, despite being a strong and independent woman. In many ways, I fantasized about being rescued as a child and because those wounds had not healed; I was continuing to live this fantasy. I wanted someone to come in and swoop me off my feet and make everything okay.

Whenever a man came into my life and showered me with love and affection, said all the things I always wanted to hear and charm me, I would fall head over heels. I thought I had finally met the man of my dreams and that my Prince Charming had finally come to rescue me. Only to experience confusion, belittling and condescending remarks, distance and what I feared was lack of interest. I would do whatever I could to recreate the experiences we had in the beginning. I would rationalize his behavior and say that he didn't mean it or he had a hard day. I would think I had done something wrong, or there was something wrong with me. I had been made to feel so unlovable as a child that I believed I needed to beg someone to love me and prove that I was worth loving.

After years of on and off again dating, with no real relationships to show for it, I again wondered what was wrong with me. I started questioning all the ways I wasn't good enough. Was I really "damaged goods'? Was I not thin enough, pretty enough, sexy enough, young enough? I was struggling to find a relationship with a good guy. I was struggling with the other relationships in my life too. In my mind, I was the common denominator, so it must be something that was wrong with me.

At one point, the belief that I would never be enough was too heavy to bear. I didn't want to live like this anymore. I didn't want to feel rejected by everyone I knew. I didn't want to feel like I would never again matter to someone else; to never have a deep, intimate and trusting relationship. Suicidal thoughts became intrusive. As is so common with suicidality, I believed that I would never be enough, I was too much of a burden on others and that I would never be accepted for who I was.

It took time and work to understand that these intrusive thoughts are old stories, and in fact, inaccurate. The truth is we will never be enough for the people who are not right for us. We may never be accepted by those who are not our people. And some people may feel burdened because they don't have the emotional maturity to hold space. The real work comes in accepting that truth and knowing that when we find the right people, we will belong, be loved and be accepted, just as we are.

WINK

I used to think that my childhood trauma was limited to the abuse I suffered at the hands of my stepdad. It took me many more years to understand that the bystanders who did nothing to help were a big reason I believed I was not worthy nor lovable. I wouldn't have discovered how disruptive my childhood experiences were had I not recognized the repeated patterns in the men I was choosing to date.

In the years that followed, after a lot of inner work, I have come to understand that if I want a different kind of relationship, I have to identify what unhealed wounds I am still trying to fix in the relationships I seek.

I had to understand what was drawing me to people, either consciously or subconsciously. It is a natural tendency to be drawn to that which is familiar, even if it isn't safe or healthy. I learned I had codependent and empathic tendencies, causing me to seek those whom I thought I could care for and fix. In turn, I believed by over-doing, over-functioning, and being needed, I would be desired.

Instead, it was a process of unlearning those beliefs and behaviors. It was about recognizing the ways in which I showed up in a relationship were the exact reasons I attracted the partners I did. I began to understand the magnetic draw that often occurs between narcissists and empaths, creating a codependent dynamic. I also started studying the importance of an interdependent relationship rather than a dependent or independent one.

Without models of healthy relationships, I leaned into the research and the self-help books. I dove head-first into every resource I could get my hands on. Initially, I believed if I could "fix" myself, then I could be lovable and desirable. What I later learned, was I was never broken, but by learning the symptomatology of these toxic relationship patterns, I could identify unhealthy traits before getting in too deep.

Activity

Self-Reflection Journal Prompts:

1. What are the common themes in your last five relationships?
2. Are there any characteristics of these relationships that remind you of the relationship(s) you have with a parent or primary caretaker?
3. What experiences from your childhood do you want to avoid repeating should you have your own children?
4. What relationship characteristics have you seen that you do not want to repeat?
5. What characteristics do you want to have in your relationships?

Chapter 5
R *is for Recognition*

5/1/2017

I feel defeated once again. It seems so easy for all the darkness to come flooding back. The pain of rejection is drowning me. I know I can come back better and stronger, but I still feel the sting of it in the moment. I want to feel wanted, appreciated, and valued. I'm sure that is what everyone wants. Now I need to pick myself up, put the pieces back together, and move forward.

I am torn to pieces and so broken-hearted. I didn't think I would see this place again. I didn't think he could cause me so much pain. Ripping my heart out after stabbing me over and over.

When asked why I stay, I fear I am not lovable and that no one will love me. I fear that the person I care so deeply for will treat the next woman so much better than he treated me. I fear losing the friendship that we have. I fear being alone and isolated. Burned, broken, pained. What I once believed is no longer.

"It is only when we understand the cycle, that we can begin to break the cycle."

Often the answers you find are not what you were looking for. Meaning, it is not uncommon for you to begin questioning why you are unhappy or is this all there is to life, only to discover that these are symptoms directly correlated to your upbringing. For me, the recognition came with the realization that I couldn't or didn't want to live like this any longer.

My husband and I sat in the dimly lit waiting room. I was feeling a mix of anger and hope, exhaustion, and despair. He sat in a chair a few feet away, his leg bouncing, as it normally did when he was anxious. I scanned the room, noticing all the various books that filled the bookshelves, the candles, and the little trinkets to make it feel a little more like home. I was doing everything I could not to make eye contact with him. We ended up in this room because he told me he didn't want our marriage to end. He was apologetic and told me he still loved me, that he would love me forever and was willing to do whatever it took. I was confused and tired of fighting so hard to make this marriage work. I didn't know what the right answer was, and I just hoped that this therapist would tell me exactly what I needed to do.

Week after week we once again sat in this room, praised for making progress, and yet I felt a rumbling of emotions inside of me because things weren't matching up. He would say everything she wanted to hear, telling her how much he was working toward this marriage and doing all the exercises. Yet we continued to have explosive arguments and I felt a complete lack of trust with him. I wasn't sure how invested I was any longer or if I really wanted this all to work out.

One day, he couldn't attend our session, so I went alone. I remember the moment the therapist leaned in a little closer to me, sadness in her eyes, and she said, "Kristina, are you familiar with personality disorders?" I nodded. She then told me she believed my husband had a personality disorder, though she couldn't quite identify which one. She recommended I do some research to better understand the signs and the effects.

With greater understanding, came greater clarity. I was finally beginning to understand the behaviors and feelings I couldn't quite put words to. As I learned more, he became more and more erratic and angry. Until the day I knew I had had enough. I met with an attorney and prepared the documents. I called my therapist, and we set a plan in place so that I could do this as safely as possible. She said she could facilitate the session while I announced that I had decided to proceed with the divorce. She would keep him for several minutes afterward to help him process the information, simultaneously giving me time to drive to a safe house.

I went into these therapy sessions seeking marriage counseling and guidance. They did not prepare me for the path that it would ultimately take me down.

Through the weeks, months, and years to follow, my therapist helped me identify the patterns I was experiencing in relationships that tied back to childhood experiences and the beliefs that I held about myself and others.

At the time of my divorce, I didn't realize how my childhood experiences had influenced the decisions I made in relationships. I didn't realize that I had so many unhealed wounds. What they don't tell you is that one giant wound can re-open so many others. I was becoming more and more aware of the toxicity of the marriage I had been in. And as I was going through the therapeutic healing process, I was also understanding that if I did not want to find myself in a similar relationship, I would have to face my wounds head on.

The deeply intertwined nature of unhealthy relationships can make it particularly challenging to recognize the dysfunction but also to end things. While you may recognize that you don't like the way things feel or you may notice that you aren't completely happy, there are good moments and positive aspects of the relationship that keep you in it. Whether you are holding out hope for things to get better or get back to the way they were, or you are fearful of what may exist on the other side of an ending, your feelings are completely normal.

To be honest, you may also find that you have similar patterns in all of your relationships. I remember asking myself, "Why does every partner of mine cheat on me?" Followed by the thoughts, "Is this normal?" "Will every partner cheat?" "How will I ever trust anyone?" We are often consciously unaware of these patterns when engaged in unhealthy relationship dynamics along with limiting beliefs and sabotaging behaviors.

If you had a dysfunctional family growing up, these patterns run even deeper. Despite what you want to call it- dysfunctional, unhealthy, toxic, etc. these dynamics seem to have an underlying pull that continues to draw you back in. When you don't have examples of healthy relationships, it can be difficult, if not impossible, to know what healthy dynamics look like and therefore you often miss or misunderstand red flags and warning signs.

Recognizing and understanding the habits and patterns in your life are an important step toward breaking the cycle. Dedicate some time to reflect on your past and identify recurring themes or patterns. Consider the commonalities in the dynamics, behaviors, and outcomes of these circumstances. If assessing relationship patterns, look for similarities in how you felt, the patterns of conflict, or the types of partners you attracted.

Observe your emotional responses and triggers within your relationships. Notice if certain situations, behaviors, or interactions elicit strong emotional reactions or feelings of discomfort. These emotional responses can provide clues to patterns that may be playing out.

Look for common themes that emerge across your relationships. These could include difficulties with trust, fear of intimacy, a tendency to attract partners with certain characteristics, or repeating similar types of conflicts. Recognizing these themes helps you understand the underlying patterns at play.

Take an honest look at your own thoughts, behaviors, and choices within these relationships. Consider if there are any patterns in how you show up, respond, or contribute to the dynamics. This self-reflection allows you to take responsibility for your role in the patterns and empowers you to make changes.

Remember, breaking unhealthy relationship patterns is a process that requires time and self-compassion. Go at your own pace and be patient with yourself as you navigate this journey of self-discovery.

WINK

I didn't realize the detriment that comes with sweeping things under the rug; nor did I understand the power that came from acknowledging and naming experiences for what they were. That was some of the initial work that had to be done in therapy. To simply recognize that the relationships I had witnessed growing up were not healthy. To recognize how I was treated and the beliefs I derived from that treatment were not healthy. And to be able to name the toxicity and trauma that resulted from my experiences of abuse and mistreatment. When you can recognize the truth, only then are you able to take adequate action to make a change.

Activity

If you haven't already done so, I recommend that you check out https://developingchild.harvard.edu/media-coverage/take-the-ace-quiz-and-learn-what-it-does-and-doesnt-mean/ and calculate your ACE score. Adverse Childhood Experiences (ACE) are common among US adults (with approximately 64% indicated a score of one or more by the time they are 18) and can indicate your risk for lasting effects on your health and well-being.

What stands out to you?

Based on the ACEs, what experiences do you believe may have impacted who you are and the relationships you engage in today?

Once you have your score, check out this resource for a list of prevention strategies:

https://www.cdc.gov/violenceprevention/aces/prevention.html

Chapter 6
I is for Information Gathering

6/2017

I actually don't know if there were obvious signs that were missed. Much of the time, when I had a feeling about something being off, I questioned him about it. Every time he denied that anything was going on, most times even accusing me of being crazy. I had asked him to stop communicating with her on multiple occasions, only to find their relationship had become stronger and more intimate over the past five years.

"The moment you start googling someone's behavior in an effort to understand it, is probably the biggest red flag you will ever need." - Unknown

When I was a child, I asked "Why" all the time. I am sure you know those kids or have seen those kids. I always needed an answer and "because I said so" was not sufficient. At one point, for a birthday, I received a book called the "Book of Why." I don't know if my parents gave that to me to get me off their back but not much has changed. I still ask why and seek to find the deeper meaning that lies beneath thoughts, feelings and behaviors. If you can relate to that, this chapter will be an exciting one for you.

As mentioned in the above chapter, when you recognize that things are not right or not what you want them to be, you may find that you ask yourself why. Why am I not happy? Why does my life look like that while theirs looks completely different? Why do I put up with the way he puts me down? Why do I keep tolerating him cheating?

When you ask enough questions, you find you have an insatiable need for answers. And so begins the rabbit hole. But remember, this time, you will go down a guided rabbit hole because you have an intention or a reason you are doing it and what you are searching for.

I don't remember where I first heard the saying, "There is almost always a why beneath the why," but it resonated. Sometimes you are too afraid to discover the truth and yet the truth will set you free. What I mean by that is your thoughts, emotions and behaviors are rooted in something deeper. When you begin to ask yourself, "Why" I want you to prepare yourself to go deep. You might not get to the root right away, for many it can take years, but if you are willing to push through the fear of what may come up, then and only then will you be able to release yourself from old stories and patterns.

Research is common in this information gathering phase to understand what you have been through, why you stayed and how to never repeat the same patterns again. Some of my earliest research related to narcissistic and codependent tendencies, people-pleasing behaviors, the rescuer and the victim archetypes and manipulation tactics. I also dove head-first into attachment theory to better understand why I felt the way I did in certain relationships.

For example, if you notice that you have a tendency to want to help others, start to ask yourself why. Is there something from your childhood that makes you feel the need to help others? Do you feel as though your value comes from others needing you? This could be a sign of codependent tendencies, which, if researched further, may provide insight into your relationship dynamics and how to break them.

Childhood experiences significantly influence the development of attachment styles. Secure attachment, where a child feels safe and supported, typically leads to healthier relationship patterns in adulthood. However, insecure attachment, such as anxious, avoidant, or disorganized attachment, can create difficulties in forming and maintaining healthy relationships. For instance, someone with an anxious attachment style may crave constant reassurance and fear abandonment, leading to clingy or codependent behaviors in adult relationships.

It is human instinct to want to make sense of things, particularly if you have experienced manipulation and gaslighting. It's important that you do not get caught up in diagnoses and labels, particularly when they have not been determined by a licensed professional. However, this information can help validate some of your feelings and may help give you guidance as you continue to seek answers.

WINK

You probably won't get the answers you need, but information helps after years of crazy-making. Unfortunately, I believe that terms like narcissist are thrown around too loosely these days. I don't say this to make light or to invalidate your experience. However, I say that because everyone has narcissistic tendencies, even though someone may not receive a formal diagnosis. I prefer to use the term tendencies because more often than not, that is what they are. You may find it helpful to identify some of the tendencies that have been identified in your past relationship(s) and then note the positives and the negatives of each.

Be cautious of blanket statements or labels, even though it may give you satisfaction in the interim. Labels can be helpful for awareness and information but can also be destructive when used to make excuses or blame.

Activity

Some of the search terms that helped me learn more about my own circumstances included: narcissism, covert narcissism, codependency, attachment theory, emotional unavailability, gaslighting, manipulation, emotional abuse, etc. Take time to understand these terms and the 'symptoms' associated with them, as they may give you clarity around your own situation.

Chapter 7
Trauma is Trauma

6/4/2017

And just like that, it all falls apart.

    I thought we were working to better our marriage, but instead I see that the blindfold has been lifted. My eyes were shielded from the fact that you weren't changing. You just wanted me to believe that you were. I am tired, too tired to fight. Maybe that is what you wanted. I may even be too tired to hurt at the moment. I built my life with you. I had my dreams of a future with you and now that has been stripped away. How foolish I was to believe the lies you told me, to fall for the show.

6/10/2017

If I thought someone had turned my world upside down before, it has now been thrown to the ground and stomped on. I am crushed, heart-broken, and shattered. To have my worst fears, my worst nightmare, become my reality. Infidelity is a wound that is indescribable; the pain, the tears, the anger, and the sadness. I missed what I thought we had, and even if by some sliver of hope we can recover from this, our marriage will never be the same. The lies, so many lies hiding so many stories. I don't know how to get past this and move on, at least not with you. This was the most painful birthday I've ever experienced. It's as if I am lost without a compass. I can't make out left from right or up from down. I am confused and unable to focus. I don't know where to go from here.

"Trauma is not what happens to you. Trauma is what happens inside you as a result of what happens to you." – Dr. Gabor Mate

People often have many misconceptions about trauma. When talking about trauma many shy away, close the book, don't want to talk about it or dismiss it because they don't truly understand what it is. Furthermore, trauma has a stigma and people do not want to be associated with the negative perceptions that may come with "getting too close" so to speak. Let's break it down for you.

Trauma is much less about the event or the situation and much more about the emotional response to that situation. While many tend to think of trauma as it relates to combat, shootings, major car accidents, and natural disasters, trauma can also apply to divorce, being bullied, or not having your emotional needs met as a child.

While I don't love labels, using Big T vs. Little t trauma can be helpful and more relatable. Big T trauma are many of the incidents listed above (combat, natural disaster, abuse, etc.), however, little t trauma should not be minimized. Little t traumas can be those things that hurt your heart even when you think back to those moments years later. Little t traumas can include getting fired from a job, breaking up, constantly fighting with your significant other, ending a friendship, etc.

The thing about trauma is that because it is not specific to the event, but rather related to the emotional response, it may not dissipate once the event has passed. The well-known and often referred to book, *The Body Keeps the Score*, by Bessel van der Kolk, MD, speaks to the ways in which memories become "stored" within our cells. Dr. Bessel van der Kolk describes how our nervous system may become hyperactive and over-protective after a traumatic event. This can activate the stress response any time the individual is reminded about their experience. It may sound extreme, however, if you have ever experienced intense stress, or trauma, you may be able to recognize some of the symptoms that may show up, even when your mind has tried to lock the memories away. Symptoms may include digestive problems, migraines, depression, anxiety, sleep issues, etc. So, when we think we should just "get over it" our survival response may not allow that to happen.

Additionally, there is research that indicates the cellular changes that can be passed down to our children and beyond. This newly discovered science of epigenetics looked at survivors of the holocaust and their descendants and discovered that some of the same changes to their genetic makeup based on stress were actually passed down generations beyond the actual event.

The research highlights the need to not just recognize the trauma but also to process and heal from the trauma. It isn't simply a matter of "putting it behind you" or "keeping it in the past" like so many try to do. If trauma and emotional responses can literally change your cellular makeup and your physiology, why would you want to carry that around the rest of your life?

Another reason to pursue healing after trauma is because there is evidence that suppressed trauma can manifest in a variety of ways, including health issues such as cancer, heart disease, anxiety, depression, and more. And last, the more you pretend that the trauma doesn't exist the more likely it is to interfere with your ability to function in relationships and in life.

Most people have or will experience trauma at some point in their lifetime. I am no exception as I have experienced a lot of trauma in my life. However, it was a long, painful journey to acknowledge and recognize it all as trauma.

The first experience in my life that I called trauma was the mass shooting at Fort Hood on November 5, 2009. I hid under my desk as gunfire popped within earshot. With the help of a soldier, my patient, I prepared to escape through my office window only to find out we were about to step out right in front of the shooter. I wailed as I ran for cover once we were given the all-clear from the police. My body shook as we waited for hours to be released and sent home. I feared we were sitting ducks, all gathered in a cafeteria-like space together, not sure where the shooter was, who the shooter was or if any and all shooters had been apprehended.

I finally made it home after midnight, twelve hours after the chaos broke out. My body was exhausted but I couldn't sleep. The next day Texas Rangers came to my apartment to interview me. I had a hard time sleeping and I had a hard time making it all make sense. I was struggling to function in my day-to-day activities, but I could the wear the mask like the best of them.

I called that event traumatic because I was finally given permission to do so. I was told that I was involved in a mass shooting, even the news reported on it day and night. I was sent to see a counselor. I was given medication and I was diagnosed with post-traumatic stress disorder (PTSD). So yes, my experience had been confirmed and validated.

And despite, or maybe because of, the validation and acknowledgment of this traumatic event, this one was the one that would haunt me the least. This one was the one I had an easier time healing from, I believe, in part, because it was a singular event and my experience was witnessed by others.

However, all the other times in my life that I later learned were traumatic, I couldn't bring myself to call them that.

There was the physical abuse that I endured as a young child from my stepdad that I considered abuse, but not necessarily traumatic.

There were times when I was told all the food in the house was for my siblings, not for me. I went to school with whatever coins I could scrape together. Occasionally there were days when I didn't have enough to afford anything, not even a pack of donuts from the vending machine. I was ashamed to ask for help, but there was an occasion or two when I asked my school counselor if she had anything I could eat. Some days she was able to get me an apple or a package of crackers. I called that unfair, but never would have considered that abuse or, God forbid, trauma.

There was the time, while on vacation, my stepdad tried to force my head under water at the pool. A little 9-year-old girl, flailing and fighting, overpowered by a very large man. Fortunately for me, though unbeknownst to my mom, she came out to the poolside at which point he finally released me.

There was the time my husband put both hands around my neck and pinned me up against the wall. He screamed in my face while I felt my airway constricting from his grip on my neck. But that wasn't abuse or trauma either because we were fighting and I believed I "deserved it."

These are just a few examples of circumstances that I would have never thought of as traumatic until, one day, I was sitting in my therapist's office and she looked at me and said, "I am so sorry that happened to you." I tilted my head a little, with a deep look of confusion because I didn't really understand. She said to me, "It never should have been this way. You were just a child and someone should have shown up for you."

Unfortunately, I learned the hard way. I thought that because I had been in therapy off and on since the age of three that I had dealt with my childhood experiences. What I didn't realize until after my divorce was there were a lot of reasons I found myself in the relationship I did. I had old wounds from childhood that I had not attended to, had not acknowledged and had not healed. These wounds, and therefore beliefs about myself, led me to become codependent, devalue myself, and engage in and tolerate toxic and abusive behavior.

Since leaving that relationship, there have been many times that I have asked myself, what if? What if I had a different upbringing? What if I truly believed I was lovable and deserving of respect? What if I had had role models to show me what a healthy relationship looked like and that it was possible?

The thing is, as Peter Crone says, "It couldn't have happened any other way because it didn't." You can grieve the childhood you had and the one you didn't get to have but your life happened the way it did. Now it is up to you to take the responsibility for healing so that you can cultivate the healthy relationships that you deeply desire and fully deserve.

WINK

I hadn't yet learned that my husband likely had a narcissistic personality disorder. I wasn't yet aware of the constant manipulation that I had fallen victim to. The gaslighting behaviors that made me feel crazy and disoriented. The name calling, bashing and mocking that came with coercion. The blame I endured for not being enough, not doing it right, and not doing what it took to keep our marriage intact.

I later learned that manipulation can be subtle in the beginning of a relationship and gradually become part of the everyday dynamic, making it more difficult to realize that it is even happening. I learned how common manipulative tactics can be and the importance of knowing the signs and setting boundaries early on to avoid falling victim to this type of behavior again.

Reflection

Think back on your life and make a list (either in a journal or in your head) about the experiences that may have been considered Big T or little t trauma. Which ones stick out to you? What emotions did you or do you feel when it comes to those experiences? Are these emotions still showing up today?

Chapter 8
Self-Care

8/13/2018

I don't feel ready right now. Not with the hurt and confusion I feel. I don't think I'm healed enough to explore new relationships. Until I feel confident that I can walk away from something or someone not deserving of me, I don't think I'm ready. I'm afraid that I will throw myself in too deep because I just want someone to want me, love me, and care for me after suffocating for so long in a relationship that wasn't that. I need to get to a place where I can stand firmly on my own two feet and feel confident being independent and on my own.

8/13/2018

I feel like so many people I loved have turned their back on me, mistreated me, or walked out on me. How can I get to a place of security and feeling like that won't be the result of my next relationship? I'm afraid I would always question someone's intentions and whether someone is being faithful.

8/19/18

I'm feeling myself becoming more comfortable and hopefully more confident. I think I'm detaching from the expectations of the relationship and gaining a better perspective and understanding of again doing what is best for me.

"An empty lantern provides no light. Self-care is the fuel that allows your light to shine brightly." – Unknown

In March 2019, I had recently arrived back home from Colombia, where I spent nine days with my mom. The relationship with my mom is not one that I would describe as a typical mother-daughter relationship. Rather than a relationship that is loving and nurturing, our relationship is defined by tension, stress, and frustration. During that trip, we argued, we pushed each other's buttons, and we were frustrated with one another on top of all the stress that can come with international travel.

Once home, I tried to take some time to rest and recover. I was watching television in the basement while watching a friend's dog. I turned everything off for the evening and began to navigate the three stories up to the bedroom. My feet felt like concrete blocks and I could barely pick them up high enough to clear the next step. It seemed to take forever to climb that first flight of stairs and the next flight was even more daunting. I tried to take one step and then the next and couldn't do it. I couldn't lift my foot high enough to take a step up. I grabbed the railing while I caught my breath. I started to cry, not because I was sad but because I was frustrated. "What now?", I thought. I didn't know what was wrong, but I knew something wasn't right. I fell to my knees and was forced to crawl up the remaining steps. Everything felt so heavy. It felt like all the energy in my body had been drained. Once I finally climbed under the covers in my bed, I immediately drifted to sleep.

A few days later, when nothing had improved, I was finally diagnosed with Epstein Barr Syndrome, which is a form of Mononucleosis. The symptoms finally made sense, but I wondered how I contracted this illness that is commonly associated with college students. Further tests revealed that I had higher than normal antinuclear antibodies, indicating an autoimmune disorder. My doctor informed me that it is typically caused by chronic and extreme levels of stress. A week later my therapist confirmed the same thing. They both told me that my body had been under so much extreme stress over the past couple of years that it was manifesting itself through illness.

One area not often talked about is the inflammation that is caused by trauma. Inflammation in the body can be detrimental and even deadly. There is research that indicates that inflammation may be a leading cause of autoimmune disorders, cardiovascular disease and dementia. Several studies conducted with Veterans diagnosed with PTSD found a correlation between PTSD and inflammatory markers. Most acute stress symptoms resolve within weeks of a traumatic event. For those who are still experiencing trauma-related stress after three months, they are often diagnosed with PTSD. When it comes to the potential for inflammation in the body, it is important to identify treatments that can help reduce or even eliminate the inflammatory effects of trauma as early as possible.

Once I was diagnosed with several autoimmune disorders, I dove deep into another rabbit hole of research, seeking answers for causes and treatments. Time and again, I kept coming back to this idea that trauma causes systemic inflammation and the best thing I could do for myself would be to reduce the inflammation through diet, exercise, and sleep.

Rest and sleep were inevitable, though, because what I wasn't prepared for was the pure mental and physical exhaustion I felt for months to come. I often designated Sundays to be my "full rest" day when I would just lay on the sofa and watch movies so that I could actually get through the following work week. I couldn't plan more than one outing in a single weekend. There were times when I would look up and want to scream, "What else are you going to throw at me? Don't you think I have proven that I am strong enough?" I wanted answers.

I wanted to fix myself so I could get to a place of normalcy that I was desperately seeking.

Like so many others, I thought self-care meant bubble baths and massages. In actuality, it is the holistic practice of taking deliberate actions to prioritize and nurture your physical, mental and emotional well-being. Little did I realize how much my fitness competition training would soon become the foundation of my healing journey.

The gym became my therapy. When I was able to sweat it out while throwing heavy weights around, I felt a cathartic release of the tension that had been building. The gym was also a place of community, where people cared about me and supported me. When my life felt out of control and chaotic, it was amazing how my prepped meals gave me much-needed structure and consistency. And when I returned home to Colorado, weekly hikes became my safe space, helping me to finally feel calm and grounded.

While the gym may not be the therapeutic space everyone needs, it definitely worked for me. It worked because I had a place where I felt confident in what I was doing. It worked because I had a routine and I didn't have to think. It worked because I was moving my body and supporting myself physically when my body had been through so much already.

Moving your body, in whatever form, helps to release beneficial hormones that can counteract those of the stress response. *With the caveat that intense or extreme exercise can actually perpetuate the stress cycle, including the flooding of cortisol, which can be counterproductive to the healing process. Your body releases endorphins which will help to boost your mood and alleviate stress. Movement gives you greater mental clarity, reduces mental fogginess, anxious and depressive symptoms, as well as boosts your mood and motivation. Moving your body is also an important part of moving emotions, so that you don't dwell on them or feel as if they are trapped. It has been proven that even twenty minutes of moderate intensity exercise or movement can have significant effects. Some studies have found that exercise can be as effective as medication and psychotherapy. The takeaway here is that any movement, for any length of time, can be beneficial to your overall healing. "When in doubt, move it out."

Research has also shown that spending time in nature induces the physiological response of relaxation, boosts immunity, decreases anxiety and depression, as well as induces protective responses against other illnesses, such as heart disease and cancer. There are many reasons for the benefits of nature but some of them include eliminating daily distractions and stressors as well as aromatic compounds that are emitted from trees and plants. Consider moving your body in nature to double the benefits.

Another area of self-care includes a proper diet. Nutritious food has a multitude of benefits that go beyond healing to include helping with mental clarity, reducing inflammation, boosting the immune system, helping heart health, giving you proper energy and more.

It is important to note that self-care is part of the holistic healing approach. Consider the areas of physical, mental, emotional, social, environmental and sleep when it comes to taking proper care of yourself.

WINK

We live in a culture that praises the hustle and grind. There is a consistent expectation that rest is for the weak. People are praised for, and wear a badge of honor for, the lack of sleep they have gotten while achieving the next big thing. What most people underestimate is the toll the stress response takes on our bodies and when lacking proper rest, this compounds over time. Like my story, the stress will manifest in a variety of ways. If you are anything like me, you may feel as though you thrive on stress, but you are, in fact, minimizing your needs and your health.

Often the most healing modalities are some of the simplest. Self-care means honoring your needs and taking care of yourself. I like to think of self-care as nourishing your body, mind and soul. Don't underestimate the power of nutritious foods, movement, spending time in nature, exposing yourself to natural sunlight and getting quality rest. Self-care can also include ways of self-soothing or finding positive habits to cope when you need it most.

Self-care means resting when you're tired. It means saying no when something doesn't excite you, instead of saying yes because you think you should. Self-care means listening to your body and responding in ways that honor your needs. Therefore, a key component to self-care is being able to recognize your needs and implementing boundaries to protect and care for yourself.

Activity

You can download a 30-day self-care bingo card by visiting www.risewithkristina.com/book1. If you get a bingo and follow the instructions, you have the chance of winning a 1:1 coaching session with me.

Chapter 9
The Blanket of Grief

8/30/20

This morning I wept. I cried and I prayed. I asked for peace and calm amid the chaos. I don't think I can bear the struggle any longer. I feel confined by challenge and heartache. I feel tormented by my lack of trust in others and myself. Sometimes it gets so heavy and so big that it is hard to remember that people love me, that people care about me, and that good people do exist. I often feel unwanted. I feel desired by the wrong people and for all the wrong reasons. I keep hearing that I need to let go, that I need to surrender and yet I feel like I can't. Maybe I'm too good at holding on. Maybe I'm too good at expectations because I dream of a better reality. My heart hurts and my pain feels heavy; sometimes too heavy to bear.

"It's an honor to be in grief. It's an honor to feel that much, to have loved that much." – Elizabeth Gilbert

It was the latter half of 2022. At this point I had already been in therapy for a couple of years after having suicidal ideations. I thought things were improving and I thought I had a good handle on healing from the painful relationships in my life.

I felt this heaviness, which I referred to as a weighted blanket, or the cloud that is always over Eeyore's head. For a few months, I noticed it but did nothing about it. I didn't say anything to anyone, including my therapist. I thought I could manage it myself and that it would go away on its own.

Five months went by and I was looking at myself in the mirror and I did not recognize the reflection staring back at me. The things I used to love doing no longer excited me. I could put on a mask to hide the pain, to function, but when I returned home, I melted into the sofa, exhausted and run down.

I tell you this because I am professionally trained to recognize depression. I am trained and experienced in mental health and even I was blind to the symptoms that I was experiencing. It wasn't until I began to once again have suicidal ideations that I knew I didn't have the strength to handle it on my own and instead I needed to reach out for help.

My therapist diagnosed me with depression and anxiety. I didn't feel anxious so I couldn't understand how I had anxiety. She and my primary care physician worked together to create a plan and put me on medication. I had been exercising and eating right but that was no longer enough. They also had me commit to reaching out if I had intrusive and suicidal thoughts again.

I believe I was depressed because I was grieving the fact that everything I thought I knew was a lie. I was grieving the reality of my childhood and the childhood that I missed out on. I was grieving the rejection and abandonment wounds that had a deep hold on me from being ostracized from my own family.

The grief process is real and even as I type these words, tears are welling up in my eyes. It was such a hard period of my life and there were times I didn't know how I would get through it. I didn't believe that I could take the pain any longer, I just wanted it all to end.

And as much as I am a believer in the holistic and natural approaches to mental health and wellness, sometimes therapy and medication are necessary supplements to everything you can do on your own.

Many of us have never been given permission to feel our feelings. I love the saying, "You can't heal what you don't feel." You may have grown up in a home where your parents didn't have the emotional maturity to handle your emotions, let alone their own. You likely didn't learn appropriate ways to manage your emotions, such as sadness and anger. As you do this work, you are grieving a lot and you may find that a lot of suppressed emotions are coming to the surface because this may be the first time you are allowing them to be expressed. For individuals who experienced trauma, you are not only grieving what you experienced but also that which you did not. Take the time and space to feel it all.

Last, aside from allowing yourself to grieve, I recommend you do not do it alone. Whether you find friends, family, a counselor or therapist, or a support group, this is a time when it is necessary to be surrounded by supportive individuals who can help you when times get tough and overwhelming.

We all experience grief in our lives. It is what we decide to do with this grief that has the potential to change the trajectory of the rest of our lives.

WINK

Grief is a powerful thing. Typically, when someone is waking up and recognizing the truth of their experiences, particularly old wounds, they simultaneously experience grief and shame. Shame is what keeps the truth buried for so long. When those memories become uprooted, so does the shame. During this time of uprooting, it is critical to practice self-compassion and allow yourself grace. Allow yourself the space and the compassion to let the emotions surface, rather than feeling the need to shove them back down.

Dr. Elizabeth Kubler Ross defined the stages of grief as anger, denial, bargaining, depression and acceptance. Unlike a video game where you master one level and move to the next, these stages may not be experienced in a linear fashion; you may toggle back and forth between the phases; or not experience a particular stage at all. You may choose to numb the pain with alcohol, drugs, mindless scrolling or binge watching, but the pain doesn't disappear. You can't outrun the grief. If you continue to numb or avoid the pain, you are never able to truly process it. Processing the pain doesn't mean forgetting or moving on but it means creating a sense of healing to remove any suffering. Even though you feel like this will go on forever, allowing yourself time to grieve is a necessary part of the healing process.

Know that grief is experienced on your own timeline. It is important to understand that we all have our own way of grieving and our own way of healing. Don't allow yourself to feel rushed through the process. Make sure you listen to your body, feel your emotions and do what feels best for you.

The grief I experienced was completely unexpected. It seemed to come out of nowhere and I could not understand it. I was not prepared for the weight it placed on me for the length of time that it did; a weight that I seemed unable to shake. I realized, once again, the need for self-care, self-compassion and grace.

Reflection

Consider where you are in the stages of grief. Or have you even begun to grieve yet? What has been the most challenging part of your grief? Where could you ask for additional support from others?

Chapter 10
S is for Self-Discovery

4/30/2017

I keep stumbling across pieces from my past. I see how dark it once was. I know there were many times I wasn't sure if I could survive it, or if I wanted to. I wish I could show my younger self where I am now. Show myself there is hope and this life is only going to continue to get sweeter. For this, I am sure, I am happy. I continue to yearn for more but in the way that I know there is greatness out there for me. There is so much yet to be discovered. There is hope.

1/2018

Decide what you want to correct in yourself that would foster more authentic, gratifying interactions.

> *Transcend the traumatic effects of your childhood.*

> *What will help me recapture my dignity, my self-respect, my sense of control in the world?*

> *Do things that make you feel valued, empowered, steady, competent, happy and proud.*

"One can only be as connected to others as they are connected to themselves." - Nicole Lapera, *How to do the Work*.

The process of self-discovery is what will lead you to self-awareness. Self-awareness is the tool that truly allows you to step back into your power. If you are a woman coming from a relationship where you felt lost, out of control, or swept up into something wild and crazy, self-awareness will be the thing that allows you to feel grounded again, knowing who you are and how to move forward.

Self-discovery is hard and it can be incredibly empowering. Looking at who we are and what we want in life can be difficult because it is often in moments of struggle and despair that we force ourselves to go inward. In those moments of curiosity (think, "How did I get it here" or "how did I let this happen to me") that the journey toward self-discovery begins. For me, as a teenager, I began my *"me-search"* (or the research to discover myself) because I believed I was flawed, and I wanted to fix myself. I believed maybe I could fix myself enough to finally be loved or accepted. This process of self-discovery sent me down a rabbit hole that has lasted for more than twenty years. Now, don't get me wrong. I wholeheartedly believe in self-discovery and self-awareness but not the pursuit of fixing yourself. You are not broken and neither was I.

We are here to learn, explore, discover and evolve. We are here to create purpose and meaning. But we need to know who we are and identify our gifts to make the most of who we are meant to be. This is the time to question everything. Ask yourself if you are living a life that you want to pursue or are you following the plans or expectations of someone else?

My second deep dive into my *"me-search"* followed hitting another rock-bottom. My divorce was probably one of the greatest blessings of my life because I could take this opportunity to explore who I was and who I wanted to be. I could take the time to play with things and figure out what I truly liked, what lights me up, and what fulfills me.

It also gave me the chance to look at what I may have been doing before others told me how I should act in order to be liked or accepted.

We all want to feel like we are part of a community, like we belong. And many of us are so desperate for acceptance that we turn to people-pleasing behaviors even if they don't align with our own authenticity.

It is quite common to lose yourself in a relationship, and after realizing that you have done so, the first question is often "How do I keep myself from ever doing that again?" This may go back to an earlier point about codependency. Or you may be someone who identifies yourself as a (recovering) people pleaser. Part of the self-discovery journey is to identify why you lost yourself in the first place. Remember, we are always going back to the root so that we can dig it up and do things differently going forward. Whether that includes healing old wounds, changing old stories, or fact checking old beliefs.

If you are willing to take a couple of minutes, I want you to honestly ask yourself these questions, "Who am I?" and "What do I want?".

When I was going through my divorce, I remember someone asking me those exact questions. I stared back at her like a deer in the headlights. My voice was shaking, and I felt embarrassed, but I responded, "I don't know". How can I not know who I am or what I want? I didn't understand how enmeshed my life had become with that of my husband.

I had lost my sense of self in that relationship. I became a chameleon and molded myself to match his wants, his desires, and his passions.

The process of discovering who I was, including who I used to be and who I wanted to be, was a long one but it allowed me to finally learn who I was at my core.

Self-awareness comprises mindfulness, reflection, introspection, observation, and emotional awareness. It helps us get to a place of knowing our identity, trusting ourselves and building unshakable confidence. Self-awareness refers to the ability to recognize and understand your own thoughts, emotions, behaviors, and patterns of thinking. It involves being aware of your strengths, weaknesses, values, beliefs, and desires. It is the act of turning inward, while also stepping outside of the self, to have a better view and understanding of what is going on. By developing self-awareness, you gain a deeper understanding of yourself and what gives your life meaning.

Research shows that having a greater sense of self-awareness results in better relationships, clarity around one's purpose, and increased well-being, self-acceptance, and happiness. When you question the quality of your life, whether you are happy, and whether you are where you want to be, you may unintentionally begin discovering who you really are. When you go deeper, you get curious about your character, your values, your beliefs and the people you have in your life.

Self-awareness can help you identify unhealthy patterns and dynamics that are or were present in your relationships. When you can step back and look at your relationships from an objective point of view, you have greater clarity around some of the warning signs and also the role you may have taken. By becoming more self-aware, you can start to break free from destructive patterns and make healthier choices moving forward.

Additionally, as you reflect, you can begin to identify patterns that were repeated from those which you observed or experienced as a child. What behaviors are you repeating that were present in the dynamic between your mother and father? What actions may be originating from beliefs that you developed as a child, based on the absence or presence of a caretaker? Or your belief about relationships and the healthy dynamic that should exist?

The ability to take time to reflect on your experiences in the relationship can be powerful. Consider how your needs and boundaries were compromised and identify any negative patterns that emerged.

Reflecting on your emotions, thoughts, and reactions can provide valuable insights.

Notice how different situations, interactions, or triggers affect you emotionally. Acknowledging and understanding your emotions can help you make more conscious choices.

Observe your own thoughts, behaviors, and patterns of interaction. Notice any tendencies to prioritize others' needs over your own, or to excessively seek validation and approval. Becoming aware of these patterns can help you make healthier choices in relationships.

WINK

Self-Awareness is one of the greatest mindfulness tools you can have in your toolbox. The ability to truly know who you are and stand unwavering and unapologetic in that power, allows you to confidently move forward. It cultivates a deep sense of self-trust and self-belief. It allows you to lean into your individuality and identity, knowing that no one can take that away from you. Self-awareness not only gives you the deeper knowing of who you are but also allows you to interact with others with greater compassion and empathy.

Activity

Self-Reflection Journal Prompts:

1. How would I describe myself to someone I am meeting for the first time?
2. What worries me most about the future?
3. What matters most in my life?
4. If I could talk to my teenage self, what would I say?
5. The two moments in my life I will never forget are…?
6. What five things make me the happiest?

Chapter 11
Limiting Beliefs

10/24/2017

I feel silly and foolish. I wonder how much I respect myself and value myself when I am so fearful of ending my relationship with you. My heart yearns for you and for us, but why? My head is so much wiser. I know that this will not work. I know I deserve so much more. I know that none of this is my fault. I know I can't trust a word you say, and yet my heart is having a hard time letting go. And no, I don't think it is a fear of being alone, but rather, I know and remember the good, fun, and loving times we shared. I know the memories we made together. You are such an enormous piece of who I am. I have lived more than a third of my life with you, and it is hard to accept this part of my life has come to an end. But I am smart enough to know that it has. I wish I could fix you. I wish I could fix this. I wish I could fix us, but I know that is beyond my capability.

12/25/20

My Christmas Wish

I wish that I knew how amazing I am. I wish I could see myself the way others see me. I feel on the verge. I feel like I am beginning to truly own who I am. I feel a greater sense of confidence and an ability to stand up for myself. I finally feel like I am understanding who I am, what I want, where I want to be and I am accepting all of it.

5/11/21

I am drowning in the unworthiness and not-enoughness. I feel my defenses go up and my armor is strengthening. Nothing feels safe. I don't know who to trust. I don't even know if I can trust myself. I don't want to feel. I'm afraid to feel. I want to numb myself to all of it. I want to purge myself of all of it and everyone. I am scared of the space I'm in. Why would anyone love me if even my own parents couldn't love me. But love is too strong of a word. Why would or how could anyone want me if my parents didn't even or don't want me? How can I be enough? Will I ever be enough? Is it even possible to be enough?

"The only thing that is keeping you from what you want is the story you keep telling yourself." - Tony Robbins

When my marriage was falling apart, my husband kept telling me that no one would love me, and no one would love me like he did. At times there was a fear that he was right. What if no one would love me? What if no one was interested in creating a life with me?

As Tony Robbins says, "Limiting beliefs are the stories we tell ourselves about who we are that keep us from becoming who we are meant to be." These beliefs come from messages we received when we were young, whether from our families, our classmates, or society. These beliefs can either be about ourselves or about the world around us.

For example, a common limiting belief that people struggle with is the feeling of not being enough. This belief is one that nearly everyone experiences at one point in their life. This belief may have been reinforced at home if you felt the need to achieve in school or in sports to get the attention of your parents. This belief is also reinforced throughout our school years with our value or worth being qualified by our grades (our grades determine where we place in the class, how we progress and where we ultimately end up going to college).

I certainly fell victim to that belief of not being enough, as well as the beliefs that I didn't matter, that I was not lovable, etc. Another limiting belief that I struggled with was that no one would show up for me, or maybe that I was not worth showing up for.

When the police showed up at my door, they walked in and began chatting with my husband. Someone asked him if he was a veteran, to which they responded, "Cool bro." When I told them that he was threatening himself and that he was threatening me, they questioned me. In the emergency room, when the attending physician asked him if he was considering harming himself or others, he denied it and therefore they had no reason to hold him. To make matters worse, the police would not write a report about the incident. This would come to have significant repercussions down the road.

After the police and the ambulance drove away, a neighbor sent me a text, "Is everything okay?" I was furious and frustrated. Everything inside of me was breaking. "Where were you when I needed someone to help me?" I called around and asked for help, but no one was willing to step in.

Similarly, I remember I was eleven years old, and I was alone in the house with my stepdad. I don't remember what I did wrong, but I remember trying to run away from him. One step, then two, then four... he grabbed my leg just above the ankle. I fell on my face as he dragged me back down the stairs. I don't remember what happened next, but somehow, I managed to break free. I ran up the stairs as he yelled after me. I locked myself in my room and got as quiet and as still as I could while I planned my escape. I packed my backpack and slowly opened my door. I could hear muffled talking as I tiptoed down the stairs making sure to avoid the one that creaked. My heart was pounding so hard in my chest I was worried it would give me away. I slid through the back glass door and ran. I jumped the fence and kept running. I ran until I arrived at the house where I babysat their kids. I knocked and banged and pleaded. The mom opened the door to see tears streaming down my cheeks but she told me she couldn't help me. She closed the door in my face. Feeling the overwhelming sense of fear and the bile rising in my throat, I didn't know what to do. This happened at three more neighbor's homes before I knew I needed to change my approach. I wiped my tear-stained cheeks with my sleeve, put on my bravest face and kept running. Out of breath, I finally arrived at a friend's house where her dad let me in so we could study together. I was safe, at least for a little while.

Growing up, I went to stay with my dad every other weekend. I have a strong memory, though I know it occurred on multiple occasions, where I complained to my dad about the treatment I received from my stepdad. My dad would get quiet, and a stern look would wash over his face. He would tell me that I needed to stop lying and immediately send me to my room for timeout once we made it home. Every time I asked for help, he invalidated me and shut me down. He made me feel ashamed for the abuse I was living day in and day out. I began to feel as though I deserved it.

Another time, I was standing in the kitchen, holding my baby sister on my hip, when my stepdad grabbed me, irate. He put his hands on my collar bone and started squeezing. It pleased him to watch me crumble under his force. My mom came around the corner and I begged her to help me. Of course, he immediately dropped his grip on me and my mom told me to stop complaining. It wasn't until later, when my little brother asked her why "daddy was pulling sister's hair" did she start to question if I was telling the truth.

I recently came across a video of me when I was about six or so. I was singing Christmas songs, as my grandmother played the piano. I could see the shy, insecure expression on my face but also could remember the feeling of satisfaction and pure joy I had any time I was able to perform. What I noticed next, sent a stabbing sensation throughout my body. As the camera panned the room, everyone else (my family) was laughing at me and mocking me. Did I have talent? Absolutely not. But I was a little girl with her heart set on entertaining those she loved with a festive song.

The feelings of being mocked, teased, and excluded as a kid carry a heavy weight. I always wanted to fit in with the other kids at school, I wanted to be liked and I wanted to be included, but I almost never was.

At home, my stepdad would taunt me and tease me, ridiculing me or making fun of something I said or did.

When I was eight years old, I was in choir and would practice our songs all throughout the house. One day, my mom told me that if I wanted to practice my singing, I had to go do it in my room, with the door closed AND locked because she didn't want to hear my terrible singing voice.

I think a lot of adults think that teasing is harmless, but it can create a lot of false stories and ultimately bruise a person's sense of self. Subconsciously, as a child, I created the beliefs that I don't matter, that I am not worthy of love, and others don't see me as valuable.

A common reason we enter and stay in unhealthy relationships is because of low self-esteem, otherwise referred to as low self-worth. When it is difficult to feel confident in who you are and deserving of love and respect, you are significantly less likely to ask for what you want and need. In this chapter, you will understand the role low self-worth plays in our relationship dynamics and patterns.

How do you define worthiness?

Worthiness, or the idea that I was worthy used to feel so gross to me. Who was I to say I was worthy? However, my idea of worthiness began to change when I had a mentor share this example with me:

Most people would agree that a baby is born worthy. A baby is worthy of love and respect, kindness and gentleness. A baby is worthy of having their needs met. Don't you agree? So then, at what point in that baby's life does their worthiness get stripped away? When do we say that a child is no longer worthy of love, respect, kindness or having his/her needs met?

In my head I used to think that worthiness meant someone who demanded respect and sat on their "throne" looking down upon others. I didn't relate it to one's basic value.

You are worthy, simply because you exist.

Trauma and traumatic experiences in relationships can deeply erode your sense of self-esteem and your sense of self-worth. Again, being able to establish and uphold boundaries can be instrumental in reclaiming and recognizing your inherent worthiness. When you assert your boundaries, you send a powerful message to yourself and others that your needs matter, and you deserve respect. This act of self-advocacy reinforces the belief that you are deserving of love, care, and consideration.

It is crucial to cultivate a positive relationship with yourself. By practicing self-care, self-compassion, and self-acceptance, you reinforce the message that you are deserving of love and nurturing, from yourself as well as others. This practice helps you to reframe negative self-talk, challenge self-doubt, and embrace your worthiness from within.

When you know your worth, you define the treatment you will accept from others. Through both boundaries and authentic communication, you create the standard that reflects your worthiness and how you expect to be treated. You no longer tolerate mistreatment or abuse, because once you know your worth you recognize that you deserve to be treated with kindness, respect, and dignity.

Furthermore, when you have a greater sense of self-worth and self-esteem you will only allow those who are supporting and uplifting to have access to you. You will begin to curate a circle of those who value and acknowledge your worthiness. When your environment changes for the positive, you develop a sense of belonging that reinforces the belief that you are deserving of genuine love, friendship, and connection. And once you are confident in your worth, you will no longer tolerate those who treat you any less.

WINK

As an adult, having the ability to reflect on past experiences, I understand how deep the pain cuts with behaviors that many think are insignificant. The song we were taught as kids, "Sticks and stones may break my bones but words will never hurt me," is so far from the truth. Words cut deep. Words can create lifelong pain and harmful stories that can influence some of the greatest decisions of our lives.

Beliefs are a feeling of certainty about what something means. Limiting beliefs, then, are the deeply ingrained thoughts or perceptions we have about ourselves that hold us back from who we really are and who we are meant to be. These thoughts and perceptions are often based on past experiences, societal influences or negative self-talk. The beliefs we hold influence how we see and act in the world around us.

Imagine your mind as a garden where your beliefs are the seeds. Just as weeds can choke the growth of beautiful flowers, limiting beliefs can stifle your progress and prevent you from flourishing. These beliefs can manifest as self-doubt, fear, or a sense of unworthiness, creating barriers that keep you from pursuing your dreams or taking risks.

These days, I am much more mindful of how I act around children, as well as the actions and words of others. It isn't to say I won't make mistakes, or I won't slip up or at times. It doesn't mean there won't be times that I let my emotions get the best of me. But I can be playful in more appropriate ways, without using words or actions that may have lasting negative consequences. This is one of the many ways we break the cycle. We no longer tolerate behaviors that had been deemed as normal or typical, no matter how destructive. We create safe spaces for our children and those kids whom we may have the opportunity to influence. We play appropriately and we apologize when we slip up.

Activity

Journal Prompts:

1. What are some of the beliefs you have about yourself?
2. Where did these beliefs come from?
3. Who's voice do you hear when you think about them?

Chapter 12
The Need to Belong

8/2020

Will I ever be enough? Will I ever feel worthy? Will I ever believe I am lovable or loved? I am struggling with all of this right now. I don't know how to get there from here. I have so many things I have always wanted. I should be happy. But I think most of all, my deepest desire is to have someone to love and to be loved in return. It all just feels so heavy, and I don't know what it is. The weight in my chest, I struggle to breathe, and I can't even identify the lesson behind it. I feel like I am always trying to prove that I am enough or that I can be lovable. I am constantly seeking approval from others. [I just want to feel like I belong.]

"I've since learned that opening up and getting hurt is a far better choice than staying closed off and alone." – Jayson Gaddis

In a single year, I couldn't imagine how so much could go wrong. I literally lost my entire family support system in one foul swoop. As I grieved this loss, and tried to trudge through the pain, I tried to uncover what actually happened. How did I lose nearly everyone I loved?

I decided that because I was the common denominator in all of it, it must be me. Once again, I faced the reality that something was wrong with me, I was a bad person and I had been abandoned by those I loved the most. After all, this was how things had been happening most of my life.

When I was three years old, my parents divorced. I may not have understood what was going on, but it was the first time in my life that I felt like I was being left behind. I didn't have the cognitive capacity to understand that my parents no longer wanted to be in a relationship. I felt as though I had done something wrong and that my parents didn't want ME.

A few years later, my mom married my stepfather, and once again my reality was disrupted. My brother arrived and then my sister. My stepdad would say things like, "We are going on a family vacation and since you aren't part of this family, you aren't invited". He frequently made comments like this to make sure he "put me in my place."

We moved around with some frequency. I only stayed at a school for a couple of years before we were on to the next. Much of the time I was okay with moving and felt like it was a fresh start wherever we went. I felt like I could reinvent myself and maybe, just maybe, be accepted at this new place. However, I always felt excluded. I was the new girl, and everyone already seemed to have their friend groups in place. So, while I was pushed aside at home, I didn't feel as though I fit in at school either. My entire life made me feel like I wasn't wanted and that I was an outcast.

As I grew older, I had a lot of affection for my younger siblings, but also observed how differently they were treated from me. They got the nice clothes and the latest toys. They went on luxury trips. They had the chance to play sports and be involved in activities with their peers. They were afforded many opportunities I was not.

Even as I sit here in reflection of this, I feel an uneasiness rising within me. I shouldn't be complaining, I should be grateful for what I had. And trust me, I know there are others who had it worse. I am grateful for the roof I had over my head and the food I had on the table. And yet I know how much my upbringing contributed to my lack of self-esteem, my belief that I am not enough and the belief that I am not worthy.

I never really felt like I belonged anywhere, because I was never really accepted, even in my own family. Over the years, this belief was continually reinforced. It has taken a long time to understand and accept I missed a lot of nurturing and love as a child. And because abandonment and rejection were so prevalent throughout my life, when my grandmother passed at the beginning of 2023, I again recognized the feeling of abandonment showing up. That is how the process works. When you are healing, it isn't that you eliminate pain or challenge from ever showing up, but you are allowed the space to observe and acknowledge. The space to hold grace for yourself and to allow yourself the time to move through the feelings while also learning how to meet your own needs in the moment.

The desire to be accepted is more than that, it is an actual human need. In tribal times, our ancestors' need for belonging and acceptance meant life or death. If you were pushed out of the tribe, you no longer had access to food, resources, or protection. While we have evolved in the generations that followed, a sense of belonging remains a fundamental need.

I moved to Florida in 2010 and was working with a group of women who regularly participated in Wine Down Wednesday. One particular evening, we decided to have a picnic at the beach. We were laughing, connecting, and telling stories about work. I am not sure what prompted me to share but I felt the urge to talk about my experience during the Fort Hood shooting. It was approximately six months after the event, and I still felt this pressure stuffed down inside of me. There were very few people I had shared the details with previously and yet it was something I thought about nearly every day. I don't believe these women were expecting to have this vulnerable conversation but something powerful happened in this experience. They had created a safe container for me to feel the emotion and to speak my truth. They sat quietly as I shared every excruciating detail and then collectively wrapped me in a hug. I knew what had happened to me but the validation I received from them not only gave me peace about my experience but also gave me comfort for all of the emotions I was experiencing in the aftermath.

Not only does community provide relief from loneliness and isolation, but there is also research that shows the true power behind validating one's experience. Countless studies have identified validation of a survivor's experience to be one of the greatest change agents to the effects of trauma. While those who were not validated demonstrated higher levels of dissociation, negative beliefs about oneself, and more severe PTSD.

For many women, it is critical that they have support throughout this decision and the aftermath. It is critical that they have those they can turn to who won't cast negative judgment. It is critical that they have a safe space. We don't always know what is going on at home. Many have become quite skilled at putting on a fun, loving, and happy exterior, myself included. Despite staying much longer than I should have, I know there is a good chance that I needed time to build my strength and confidence, along with a personal support system, to walk away successfully. If you can hold the safe space for another, let them know. Maybe they aren't going through anything challenging, but maybe they are. Everyone, survivors most of all, just want to feel seen, heard and accepted. Those who created that space for me literally saved my life.

As Jayson Gaddis once said, "If you remain closed off out of fear, you also miss out on the beauty that comes from being open."

WINK

Community is a vital piece of healing. The ability to have safe spaces where you can be yourself, lean on others for support and be validated in your experience is critical.

I didn't realize that my strength and my independence, characteristics I prided myself on, were, in fact, a trauma response. Hyper-independence, those moments where you say or think, "I don't need anyone. I am good on my own" tends to come from a place of trauma and survival. Rather than strength, it is a protective mechanism that is put in place to avoid being hurt, abandoned, or rejected once more.

Understand that you aren't serving yourself when you close yourself off to deep connection with others. Community (and the right community) helps you heal but also serves as a protective mechanism against future challenges.

I often hear women say that it is just too hard to meet people. Find activities you enjoy doing and attend them in person, even if you are scared to put yourself out there. I have met some of my best friends at events (both in person and online) when I was willing to do the thing that felt most uncomfortable.

Activity

List 3 people who you can turn to in difficult situations:

1. _____

2. _____

3. _____

Identify 1-3 events/places you can attend in the next month to meet new people (i.e., a mom's group, the gym, a class, etc.):

1. _____

2. _____

3. _____

Chapter 13
Authenticity

3/2018

I am still having a hard time answering the question of who I am. Maybe I'm not meant to. Eckhart Tolle says the answer is simply: I am. Everything that I used to define myself and my identity has been stripped away. I used to say that I was an OT, a researcher for the Department of Defense, a homeowner and a wife. I identified with those things for so long I don't know who I am without them. I don't feel as though I have [anything that defines me] anymore.

Who are you when the things you have used to identify yourself or stripped away? Whether it was a person or a position?

I am not my roles. I am much deeper than that. But it took losing those roles to become awakened to it. Honor the function without becoming identified with the function. We are not the ideas in our head.

You can't fully be yourself if you don't know who you are.

"Trauma disconnects us from ourselves because it would be too painful to feel so small." – Peter Levine

How often do you hold onto old labels such as that of a college athlete or defining yourself by the degree you earned in school? How often do you prioritize your accolades over your character?

In this book, you have read about the loss of identity and the loss of oneself in relationships. As I have mentioned before, two of the most difficult questions to answer after you have experienced manipulation or abuse, or if you have a tendency to put the needs of others before your own, are "Who am I?" and "What do I want?"

I remember when my marriage ended, I had lost all sense of who I was. I felt like I had the rug pulled out from under me and I was treading water just to keep my head afloat. I used to define myself as a wife, a homeowner, a researcher, an innovator, a career woman, a dog mom, a Florida resident, etc. In the blink of an eye, I was no longer any of those things. Due to the safety concerns amid my divorce, I had to move across the country. Not only did that mean ending my marriage and selling our home, but it also meant leaving everything I "knew" behind, including my career, my friends, my neighbors, my weekly routines, etc.

I felt lost. I didn't know who I was, and I was filled with dread every time I was asked that question. But one day, I had the realization that if I was no longer those things, I had a blank slate in front of me. I had a new opportunity to define who I wanted to be and in doing so, release the labels that could be so easily taken away.

I realized that my previous identity had been wrapped up in labels and external ones at that. I realized those labels were the masks I wore. They had everything to do with the way others perceived me or how I wanted to be perceived, but nothing that actually had to do with who I was as a person.

Instead, I wanted to be Kristina, the woman who is kind, happy and radiates warm and welcoming energy when she walks into a room. The woman who people feel drawn to and want to know because there is something different about her. The woman who is confident in who she is and isn't afraid to step into that fully. The woman who cracks a joke often because she doesn't take life too seriously. The woman who is calm and at ease and helps others feel safe in her presence. The woman who feels so good about herself that she gives others permission to fully be themselves even without a spoken word.

So, my question for you is, if you don't know who you are or how to define yourself in this moment, who do you want to be? What do you want to be known or remembered for? How do you want to make others feel?

I spend a lot of time addressing identity because I feel that it is one of the most meaningful pieces of our lives. The clearer you can be about who you are and what you want in your life, the greater ease and flow you allow as you cultivate the life you deserve and desire. When you have clarity around who you are, you can be authentically you., and you realize the power that comes with being unafraid of all that you are.

The meaning of authenticity is being true to your values, personality and spirit, despite the outer circumstances. Authenticity can be both powerful and liberating as it involves embracing and expressing your true self without fear or inhibition. The more comfortable you are with yourself, the more confident and certain you are in your relationships. You create spaces where you can be true to yourself and let go of the masks you may have worn in the past.

WINK

Trauma disconnects us from who we really are. Understand that you had to become the person you did in order to survive. You may have had to play a role so that you were accepted by your "tribe" so to speak. You may have had to hide certain parts of yourself for fear that you would be an outcast. There is nothing wrong with that because it was what you needed then. But it is your responsibility now to connect back to yourself.

Activity

Two exercises I like to use with clients to help them identify these things are values and characteristics exercises. Sometimes it can be challenging to come up with how you want to be defined without some tangible examples. Therefore, both of these exercises can help you pinpoint characteristics and values that resonate most with you.

Now consider the question, "What do you want?" Again, depending on your life circumstances, you can look at this as a blank slate. I know that reframe was incredibly beneficial for me as it helped me focus on the positives of the situation rather than the negatives.

Here are some questions to help you get started: (If it feels safe and comfortable to do so, allow your younger self to come alive in these questions. Let it be playful and let your imagination come to life. Don't worry about the how or if this would even be possible. Allow yourself to dream as big as you can, and you want).

1. If you could live anywhere in the world, where would you live? Would you live in a specific city, state or country? Would you live in the mountains, on a lake, at the beach? Would you live in a high rise, in a suburban neighborhood or in a cabin? Let your mind run free.
2. What would you do to earn money?
3. What is most meaningful in your life? How can you create more meaningful moments?
4. What types of relationships do you want to have? What would it feel like when you are around those types of individuals?
5. How do you want to spend your free time?

Chapter 14

Boundaries

11/2021

I feel like there is so much swirling in my head right now. I am [trying to process] the relationship dynamics with my family. I don't believe the relationships are aligned for me any longer. As much as I love Christmas, I don't want to participate this year. I'm tired of trying to be so perfect to prove myself and feel connected to my own family. I'm over allowing myself to be treated like I don't matter or that I'm not enough.

3/5/2022

Dear Dad,

The change in our relationship has caused me a lot of emotional distress and heartache. I don't know what caused the disconnection, but it has been a really difficult time for me. I don't feel like I have my dad when I wanted and needed a father. I need some time to figure out the best and healthiest way forward for me, and us.

Sometimes the hardest endings are with family, not lovers.

"The only people who get upset when you set boundaries are those who benefitted from you having none." – Unknown

After returning to Colorado, I was hoping for a safe place to land. I was back with my family and, maybe without even knowing it, needed to be embraced and loved. Living in Colorado in the months prior had reaffirmed that this was where I was meant to be. And yet, less than a month after leaving my job and officially leaving Florida, I was confronted by a family member.

I was cornered, and with no witnesses around, she unleashed her wrath on me. She told me I was the greediest person she knew. She told me that I made everyone around me feel uncomfortable and feel as though they had to walk on eggshells. She told me that she had resented me since I was seven years old while she preached to me about God and grace.

I sat there, on the sofa next to her, and crumbled. I cried so hard that snot was running down my face and into my mouth. I was choking and unable to catch my breath. She told me I needed to be grateful for what I had, take a deep breath, and put a smile on my face.

I could hardly believe what had just happened. My eyes were almost swollen shut and I couldn't think clearly. I wasn't sure how I would drive home but I knew I couldn't stay there one more night.

On the drive, I allowed her words to sink in a little deeper. I was struggling with the idea that she could be so harsh and also struggling with the idea that she resented me as a little girl. I was an innocent child, and I couldn't make her words make sense.

In the years that followed she frequently shared the story about how much she sacrificed for me. She said it was not the life she had envisioned for herself.

I tried to confide in my dad, only to find myself invalidated once more. Why would I expect him to believe me now, when he never had before?

I distanced myself further from them. I knew that I would not tolerate this kind of treatment from a friend, so why would I from my family? I stopped receiving invitations for dinner and I stopped attending holidays with the family.

I had finally gotten to a place where I admitted to my dad that I did not want to see him and needed time and space. He didn't understand where I was coming from but knowing how infrequently he was reaching out, it wouldn't be hard to get the space I was requesting. Unbeknownst to us, we were nearing the final few months of my grandmother's life.

This ending threw us all back into a strange mixed soup of sorts. We were trying to navigate the awkwardness of our relationship while trying to support one another and soak up the precious time with my grandmother. After she passed, I had the realization that once again, I was finally free. There was nothing holding me to them any longer. Just like when I ended my marriage with my ex, I now had the freedom to do life on my terms and only allow those in my life who respect me and love me for the person I am.

It would often "trigger" me that when I shared about the grief I was struggling through each day, people automatically assumed I was referring to a romantic relationship. The deepest grief I have ever felt came from trying to understand, and maybe even justify, the relationship, or lack thereof, with my dad.

No matter how hurt I felt by him, that little girl seeking daddy's approval and love always seemed to burst to the surface. The little girl who would do anything to prove that she could do whatever it took to earn his love, was always there, ready to perform. There were more than a few times that I sat on his driveway and cried while explaining to him that I only wanted to make him proud. I only wanted to prove that I deserved his love. And yet it was never enough.

Trying to do the dance of healing, meeting my own needs, accepting I would never be able to get what I needed from my dad, and learning to protect myself through the use of boundaries, led to some of the most challenging time of my life. Several years prior I had set similar boundaries with my mom, but it never became the emotional struggle that I seemed to entangle me and my dad.

Boundaries are a part of speaking up and advocating for yourself. They define where you begin, and another person ends. Boundaries and needs go hand in hand. You have to be able to recognize what you need to set boundaries. You determine what you will and will not allow in your life based on your values, beliefs and needs. If you need space, you must be able to acknowledge that need, ask for that need to be met, and then stay firm when it comes to honoring that need.

Boundaries can be really challenging for someone who was once told their needs don't matter. Or someone who was so desperate to fit in that they put everyone else's needs first at the detriment of their own. More often than not, you may fear putting boundaries in place because you fear how others will think/feel about you, or even worse, you fear that you will be abandoned or rejected. The truth is boundaries are healthy and necessary in your relationships.

I frequently think of a pendulum in many areas of the healing journey. When setting boundaries, I found that I would swing wildly from one extreme, of no boundaries, to the other extreme of becoming very firm and rigid. When first learning how to enforce them or how to protect yourself as you heal, you may need to begin with more rigid boundaries before you can allow them to soften with time. There is no hard and fast rule when it comes to your boundaries, but rather they are dependent on your needs and your ability to stand firm in what you need. Understand that boundaries may shift over time and boundaries will likely look different for different people and in different contexts within your life.

Establishing healthy boundaries will allow you to regain a sense of control, rebuild your self-worth, and create a safe space for yourself. Boundaries can be broken into four different categories.

First and foremost, setting physical boundaries is essential. This involves defining your personal space and deciding who is allowed into that space. It means having the power to say no to things that make you uncomfortable and asserting your right to control the energy around you.

Relational boundaries include identifying and limiting contact with individuals who have been toxic or abusive in the past. It means being selective about who you allow into your life and setting clear expectations for how you should be treated. It also involves creating distance from individuals who consistently invalidate or manipulate your feelings. By setting relational boundaries, you can create healthier and more fulfilling relationships that nurture your growth and well-being.

Last, it is necessary to incorporate boundaries around your self-care practices. This includes recognizing your capacity, prioritizing your own needs, and giving yourself permission to engage in activities that promote healing and well-being. It means setting aside time for self-reflection, therapy, or engaging in hobbies that bring you joy, contentment and peace. By establishing self-care boundaries, you will begin to rebuild your sense of self and regain control over your life.

To set boundaries, it is important to identify where you have boundaries in place and where you may be lacking. Consider what activities or people add or detract from your overall experience. Once you can identify areas that need improvement, determine what is important to you and what you want from various relationships.

Boundaries might look like:

- Scheduling time for your own self-care.
- Identifying the length of time you are willing to attend a gathering and planning your exit strategy.

- Deciding to call or text someone rather than meet up face-to-face.

Boundaries might sound like:

- I won't be able to come out tonight. I need some time to recharge.
- I don't feel comfortable speaking about my relationship.
- I am feeling really isolated, would you be able to meet up for coffee tomorrow?
- I feel unheard when I voice my concerns. Could we set some time aside to talk about it, without distractions?
- Simply saying "No."

Boundaries might feel like:

- Allowing your body to rest when you are tired.
- Once in place, you feel a weight lifted off your shoulders.
- You feel a greater sense of peace and ease.

It is important to note, however, that boundaries will likely feel uncomfortable at first. You may experience anxiety around the reactions you may receive from others. Others may push back. Often, those who are unhappy about your boundaries are those who never respected you in the first place.

That being said, boundaries are essential for women who are survivors of trauma and toxic relationships. They provide a framework for self-protection, empowerment, and growth. By setting physical, relational, and self-care boundaries, you can create a safe and nurturing environment that supports your healing journey and helps you reclaim your life.

WINK

Unfortunately, disregarding your own needs can be a complex issue with roots that tie back to societal or family expectations, low self-esteem, manipulation, and beliefs. Breaking free from this pattern requires support, empowerment, and a reclamation of your own self-worth. It involves recognizing the importance of self-care, establishing boundaries, seeking help, and ultimately prioritizing your own well-being and happiness.

Activity

Get clear on the relationships where you may need to set boundaries using the questions below. Start first by identifying the top 5-10 people you spend the most time with and then use the following questions for each.

1. What type of relationship is this? Is this a family member, a partner/spouse, a friend, a coworker, etc.
2. When thinking about this person, how do you feel?
3. Are you always or nearly always excited to spend time with or talk with this person?
4. Who initiates connection, whether in person or over the phone?
5. Does the energy feel reciprocated in this relationship?
6. What are the top 3-6 emotions you feel after connecting with this person, i.e., at peace, excited, resentful, exhausted, angry, fulfilled, happy, etc.?
7. Would you prefer to spend more or less time with this person if there were no consequences or barriers?
8. Do you believe you need to implement boundaries with this person? If so, what might they be?

Chapter 15
Rebuilding Trust

7/2020

My current fears are twofold- can I trust myself and can I trust others?

I know I am not a victim but rather a contributor to my past situations and experiences. What do I need to learn or unlearn going forward?

I'm confused. Was I totally blindsided? Was I lied to? I feel like I saw a very different person the last two weeks than who I believed him to be or thought he could be. This is very reminiscent of my marriage. I'm relieved to have the revelation so early on and the willingness to stand up for myself but also sad, frustrated, and fearful to fall so hard for someone only to have it turn out the way it did.

7/2020

I feel like there is a lot to work through around trust. Trusting myself and others. I know I'm getting better about trusting my intuition and standing up for myself, but I am still angry, hurt and feel like a fool. How could I have been so foolish to fall for his words? How could I have been so foolish to fall for him the way that I did? He hurt me in ways I truly believed he couldn't or wouldn't. I believed he wanted the best for me. I believed he was there to protect me and keep me safe. I'm so angry with myself for believing in him as much as I did. I'm sorry I saw the best in him, it led me to a broken heart and disappointment.

"Being able to feel safe with other people is probably the single most important aspect of mental health; safe connections are fundamental to meaningful and satisfying lives." – Dr. Bessel van der Kolk

For me, learning to trust after all that I had experienced was one of the most challenging processes, and honestly still is. While I feel as though I have a good grasp on many areas of my healing, trust continues to be a sticking point for me.

Trust is formed in infancy. That is the time we determine whether the world is safe, whether we can trust that our needs will be met, to trust that we will be heard and cared for, and more. Our trust can be shaken at any time, however, the foundation of our trust and how we perceive the world around us is formed in the first years of our lives.

When you learn to trust that the world is good, that the people around you are good, and that your needs will be attended to, you have this underlying expectation that it will be so. However, once your world is shaken, it can be incredibly difficult to rebuild that trust again.

Our ability to trust is also what leads to our attachment styles for our future relationships. If we had a healthy response from our caretakers, we will have an innate trust in others and feel secure in our relationships.

As a child:

1. Could you trust that your parents would have food on the table each night?
2. Could you trust that you were safe in your own bed?
3. Could you trust your parent to comfort you when you were sick or if you fell off your bike and scraped your knee?

In your relationship(s):

1. If a friend, a partner or a parent were to ask to borrow $100, do you trust that they will repay you?
2. If your car were to break down on your way to work, is there someone you could call, who you trust will answer the call and help you out in a bind?

3. Do you trust a friend, partner or parent enough to call them and talk about how you truly feel, without fear of judgment or dismissal?

Your response to the first three questions will greatly inform the underlying "why" for your response to the latter three. If you confidently responded "yes" to the first, you likely have security in relationships, and therefore a secure attachment. This sense of security allows you to have a deep sense of trust in those around you.

If you responded with an adamant, "Nope" or you were on your own to fend for yourself, you have likely developed a sense of hyper-independence. This type of conditioning will lead to an insecure attachment style and one where you don't feel as though you can trust or depend on others, so you will just take care of things yourself.

And if you are unsure or there was inconsistency in the availability of those you depended on, you will have likely developed an insecure, and more specifically, an anxious attachment style.

Whether obvious or not, your childhood has had a significant impact on who you are and how you engage with others around you. This also affects how you subconsciously expect your partner to behave, and therefore, how you respond.

Trust is twofold and requires you to trust yourself and to trust others. What I have come to learn is that self-trust is foundational and by far, the most important. This is where becoming familiar with your intuition is critical. It is also necessary to prove to yourself that you have your own back. There is always going to be a trust-building process with others, however, when you can trust that you can rely on yourself to keep you safe and make the right decisions, you know that it will all be okay. When you rebuild trust within yourself, you become more confident in your decisions, actions, and abilities.

When you begin to analyze your relationship(s), you can identify red flags that you may have dismissed or minimized. You can also begin to examine the patterns and dynamics of those previous relationships. What things showed up repeatedly? What did you ignore and why? When you can begin to identify the reasons why you may have missed behaviors or tolerated behaviors, you can acknowledge the changes you can make to protect yourself in the future. This self-awareness serves as a protective measure and allows you to establish boundaries that safeguard your trust.

As scary as it may be, learning to trust others requires embracing vulnerability. You must cultivate a supportive network of individuals who have proven themselves to be trustworthy and reliable. When you find the types of people who you feel comfortable and safe sharing your stories with, and you are validated in your experiences, you will begin to rebuild trust in others. These healthy connections foster a sense of safety and reinforce the belief that there are trustworthy people in the world.

Boundary-setting is another critical part of rebuilding trust. When you set a boundary, and you uphold that boundary, you begin to rebuild trust in yourself. You begin to learn that you have got your own back. When you set a boundary and another person respects and honors that boundary, you begin to build trust in them. These boundaries serve as a framework for trust, allowing you to feel secure and in control of your interactions with others. The more often you witness the respect and validation of your boundaries, you can begin to trust that your needs will be honored.

Ultimately, rebuilding trust after trauma is a complex and deeply personal journey. It requires time, patience, and self-compassion. By combining self-awareness, vulnerability, healthy connections, self-trust, and boundary-setting, you will begin to gradually restore your ability to trust others and, most importantly, yourself.

WINK

The idea of trusting someone again was overwhelming. I wasn't sure if I could ever get to that point. I am much more skeptical than I have ever been, but I keep reinforcing my self-trust because that is all I have control over. I regularly do things that prove that I am reliable, dependable, safe, and consistent for me. That is all I can do, and I hope you learn that you have that power too.

Activity

Identify three promises you will keep to yourself this week. When you show up for yourself, you rebuild self-trust. Examples might be: "I will take a 10-minute walk outside every day', or "I will drink a glass of water first thing in the morning." Make sure to create 3 promises that count toward self-care and are meaningful for you.

1._____

2._____

3._____

Chapter 16
Listening to the Nudges

6/23/2017

Shock, disbelief, anger, sadness and hurt all the questions
    I still don't know why
    I never expected this to happen to me or to us
    where is my pride in my decision
    am I valuing myself worth
    is this fixable
    is this even worth fixing
    is love enough?

10/23/2017

So much has happened over the last week, more than I could have imagined. Except for the fact that my intuition told me everything. I was prepared every step of the way—from finding your emails professing your undying love, to seeing the phone records showing that you started calling her the day after you moved out, to the incessant messaging, [and even] breaking into the house. I know this isn't you, yet at the same time, I know enough about you to have predicted it in some way. I filed for divorce on Thursday. Despite the concrete evidence that I needed to be 100% certain of my decision, I broke down when I received notification that it had been filed. Even as I try to put on a calm and strong front, I am breaking inside. I love you, and I am sure a part of me will always love you. I have learned, though, that love isn't enough.

6/25/2018

I've been challenged lately with the two mindsets of "face your fears" and "trust your gut." My gut has been telling me "danger" but I didn't want to regret not giving Tampa a chance. So here I am, and my body, more than ever, is telling me to turn and run away as fast as I possibly can. I've been physically ill. I've had nausea, paranoia, extreme fear and discomfort, and I've been overwhelmed with emotion. I love what I do, but I can't put myself through this any longer.

"Woman's intuition wasn't intuition at all, it was heightened observation, unconscious registration of subtle clues." – Orson Scott Card

One year after investing heavily in personal development, I was no longer the same person. The veil was lifting, and I understood that I had a choice to make; I could either continue to live life as a victim and deal with the blows as they came, or I could take responsibility for the life I wanted to live. I would no longer allow life to happen to me and if it were to take me down, I would go down with a fight.

I poured everything I could into creating a life I wanted to live. I had taken back control of my health. I was applying for my dream jobs, and I was investing in marriage counseling to salvage what I could.

One day, I noticed a weird phenomenon. I started seeing repeating numbers on the microwave and then on the clock in the car. Once I noticed them, I couldn't un-notice them. Initially, I thought they were a sign from my cousin that he was present with me through whatever challenge I would face. But then they were everywhere, all the time. I shared some of these sightings with my husband and he asked, "do you think it means you are supposed to leave me?" I contemplated this for a few seconds and responded, "I won't pretend I know what they mean, but I do believe they mean that I need to slow down and pay attention."

This was the reinforcement I needed to start paying attention to my intuition, knowing that when it was nudging me, I needed to listen. And when I say start, I mean it was a long process to get me where I am today and even still, I am nowhere near where I would like to be.

It started with every once in a while, saying, "huh, I feel you" and yet I didn't always listen. I had ignored the feelings for far too long, partly because I thought they were nothing and partly because I was called crazy any time I questioned it. It is amazing how outside forces can detach you so greatly from your greatest gift and your greatest compass. In the way that we sever our deepest, realist truth to belong to and be loved by the people we allow in our lives.

Once I started acknowledging it again, the tap, tap, tapping came more often and sometimes more fiercely. I love the saying that if you ignore the nudges, you will eventually have to face a 2x4 to the head. It is up to you how long you want to ignore the truth, but you can't ignore it forever.

Thank goodness I began to listen again because I truly believe that listening is what saved my life more than once in the coming months.

It can be difficult to differentiate intuition from fear, particularly when your feelings are consistently invalidated. How often have you heard, or even thought to yourself, "I had a feeling..."? The more I worked and poured my energy, time and finances into making the marriage work, or at least knowing that I gave everything I could, the more my gut told me that things weren't right. When I tried to confide in others or seek input, I was consistently told I was imagining things, or worse, that by focusing on my fears, I was, in turn, creating a self-fulfilling prophecy. I began collecting evidence, just to prove that I wasn't crazy, not only to my husband but also to my friends and family who doubted me.

Once I had sufficient evidence of the truth, I felt justified in my decision to proceed with a divorce. I contacted an attorney, filed the paperwork, and reached out to my therapist to assist me with the conversation that needed to occur with my husband. My intuition told me this would not be a safe situation, and, despite the doubters, I finally trusted myself. I made a plan, packed my bags, set up the necessary arrangements and went into hiding, the first of several times to follow.

A few weeks later, after returning to my home, I woke up to 42 text messages on my phone. My heart sank and my stomach turned in knots. My gut told me something wasn't right. I brushed it off, figuring he wouldn't really do anything. And yet, I am pretty sure my lizard brain (the one that acts in times of survival) was smarter than the logical part of my brain that day. I sat down on the sofa with my hot cup of coffee and turned on the television. Before long, I jumped at the sound of pounding and shouting on the other side of the door. I told myself I needed to keep it together and put on a brave face while I stepped onto the porch to prevent him from trapping me inside. I let him fall apart, standing there while he screamed and yelled at me, begging, pleading, and threatening to take his life, as well as my own.

I calmly told him there was no turning back; I had made my mind up, and we were getting a divorce. As he stormed away, I followed behind him and snapped a photo of his license plate so I could provide it to the authorities. I wasn't sure what he was going to do, but I knew he was not thinking clearly, and I knew he was not safe.

I made it back inside my home and locked the front door. I tried to dial out on my cell phone, but it wouldn't connect. I went to the home phone and, oddly, there wasn't a dial tone. Suddenly, I heard more pounding, this time beginning at the garage door and almost as if I were in a movie, I froze in place and followed the sound around the side of the house. The phones were not connecting. I couldn't call for help. I caught myself before falling into a full-blown panic. I ran to the keypad for my home alarm and immediately armed my house.

Two months prior, I had again followed my gut and decided I needed to boost the security of my home, including the addition of glass break sensors. I may have even forgotten that they were there as I watched him move to the back patio. Once again, he was screaming at me, yelling that he was going to kill me. He started kicking the glass French doors. The glass splintered and then, one piece at a time, popped into the house. I yelled back at him to stop, telling him I would just let him in. But he kept kicking and kept kicking. The glass fell to the floor, and he walked through. A monster was in my home, telling me he was prepared to take my life, and all I could do was calmly order him to sit on the cold tile while I rushed to get him wet rags for his bleeding leg and a glass of water.

The phone rang and when I answered it, I felt immediate relief in learning that the glass break sensors had alerted the police. They gathered my information, told me they would send someone out and hung up. Yes, the dispatcher hung up on me after my husband had just broken into my home, threatening to kill me and himself. I immediately dialed my dad, and he told me to keep him on the phone until the police arrived.

Once he was loaded up into the ambulance and headed to the hospital, I knew I had a limited amount of time before he was released. Again, I scrambled to get my stuff together, make arrangements for the door to be fixed and leave town. This was the day I realized a go-bag would be a part of my future going forward. I may never know when I might have to flee my home in fear of my own life, but I had a feeling this wasn't the last.

A month or so later, my husband reached out to ask if we could meet to discuss the terms of the divorce. I wanted to agree to his request as I wanted this to be an easy and respectful process, regardless of the pain and the fear that had become a standard part of my everyday life. And while I wanted to honor him, my gut was again pinging. I knew I could not meet him in a private place because I couldn't trust him, his temper or how he may react. I gave him the name of a nearby restaurant where we could meet. When I saw him, I couldn't understand what I had been so afraid of. He was familiar and he was someone I had loved. We worked our way through the tension, trying to find things to talk about, knowing that harder conversations were coming.

I don't remember what we said, but I witnessed something I thought only existed in horror movies. His rage returned, but this time, instead of looking like a pot beginning to boil, his eyes turned black. They were empty and simultaneously full, seething with what felt like evil and hatred. They were something unrecognizable in them and it sent a chill down my spine. I hadn't felt fear like that before. Fear because I was sitting in a restaurant, surrounded by other people, knowing the thinnest space that existed between my survival and my death. Observing him cold as stone as I sat there, motionless, speechless, unable to take my eyes off him, silently willing him to come back to his body.

WINK

Over the years, I have learned to know when my intuition is telling me something. I have also realized there is a difference between acknowledging that feeling, listening and honoring. If you don't do all three, you are shutting down the greatest gift you have.

Your intuition doesn't just speak to you about negative or scary situations. Again, being the greatest gift, your intuition can guide you to seek and find opportunities you may not otherwise. For example, I followed the pings of my gut to go on a solo trip to Portugal. It almost felt like it was calling to me and at the time I would not have known the beautiful bonding experience it created for my grandmother and myself just before she passed unexpectedly.

I have also learned to trust my gut when I feel pulled to attend certain events and haven't regretted it. I have met so many incredible people by going to a dinner, a networking event, a conference, just "because I had this strong feeling" to do so.

Reflection

The practice of following your intuition is like a muscle that becomes stronger the more you do it. The first part requires tuning in, while the second requires you to listen.

Do you remember a time, earlier in your life when you ignored your intuition or that gut feeling? Trusting your intuition may not always be a life-and-death situation, but if you don't know what it feels like to listen and then honor that feeling, what happens if the situation is that dire?

Chapter 17
The Power of the Mind

12/31/2019

Every lesson learned, every earth-shattering heartbreak, every experience, every win led me to this moment. Time and again I proved to myself that I could accomplish anything I set my mind to. Through the highs and lows, the trauma, the losses, the obstacles, the rainbows, the beauty and the achievements, it was a decade of unexpected outcomes. Despite the multiple trials of rock-bottom darkness, I wouldn't change a thing. For if I hadn't endured the hardships, I would not be experiencing the beautiful magic of all that I have in my life today. Remember this: We cannot predict the future. We don't control the way our lives unfold. How many people are saying, "I never could have imagined but...". Stay present in the moment; know that you create your reality and manifest your desires; and be open to receiving all the divine goodness that is meant for you.

"The only limit to our realization of tomorrow will be our doubts of today." – Franklin D. Roosevelt

Mindset is defined as a set of beliefs that influence the way we think and act in the world.

I hear a lot of gurus and teachers say, "Your mindset determines your reality" and I used to believe that too. The common analogy is the following:

Let's say you wake up late. Your alarm didn't go off, and you jump out of bed in a panic. You rush to the bathroom only to stub your toe on the corner of the wall. Then you forget to grab your lunch as you hurry to the office. In the car, you get stopped at every red light. Meanwhile, you feel your blood boil. You are angry and cutting people off as you change lanes because you can't be late to work today, you have a huge presentation. At the next red light, you yell some words of frustration and say, "Of course this would happen to me today." This anger and frustration follow you throughout your day. You are rude to your colleague who makes a joke that you are late. You find yourself flustered for your presentation and so on.

You can see how this domino effect falls into place. The idea is that when you look for the negative, you will find it. More recently, a friend of mine shared the quote, "Your mindset doesn't determine your reality, it determines the way you experience your reality" and I think that feels more appropriate.

The lens through which you choose to see is what you will find and have reflected back to you. When you are focused on the negative aspects of life, of your job, of your relationship and so on, you will continue to see and be presented with negative situations. Whereas, when you choose to focus on the positives, you will in turn experience a lightness and more things will seemingly go your way.

Now, don't get me wrong here. I am not saying that if you simply change your mindset and focus on the positives while in a toxic or abusive relationship, you will fix things. I fell into that trap for some time, and it does not work. However, the more I focused on the positives within myself and my life, the more I was able to convince myself that I could walk away from that relationship and know that I would be okay.

To do that, though, you must believe that things can change. If you have a fixed mindset, you are likely to believe that you are a victim of circumstance and that you are unable to change your situation. Whereas if you have a growth mindset, you believe that you have the ability to change, despite your circumstances. One way of thinking, the fixed mindset, will keep you trapped in a life that isn't serving you. While a growth mindset opens the door to your potential and gives you access to your own freedom.

The fixed mindset is one of limitations, often described as a belief that you are born with certain strengths and weaknesses that are unable to be changed. Or life has dealt you a bad hand or that you "made your bed and now you have to lie in it."

The growth mindset is one where a person believes they can continue to learn new information and new skills to change the way they interact with and in the world around them.

If you believe that you can change and grow, you can open a world of possibilities. You can believe that while you may have been a victim of abuse, or the subject of mistreatment, or even participated in an unhealthy relationship, a victim mindset doesn't serve you.

Acknowledging what was and what happened while believing in more is what will help set you on this future path to creating the life that you may not even believe is possible right now.

Like mindset, words matter. The more you repeat certain words or phrases, the more they become your regular thoughts which then turn into your beliefs.

If you continue to tell yourself you can't do something, you are right. Whereas, making even a simple shift to something like "I think I can" you may surprise yourself.

How long did you believe you couldn't leave a toxic relationship? "I can't leave because we are married." "I can't leave because we have kids together." "I can't leave because what will others think of me?" The belief that you can't is what will keep you stuck. If instead, you think of ways that maybe you can, you begin to open the aperture through which you are looking. You will begin to see new options and new opportunities that you couldn't see before, when you had a narrowed focus.

What words do you consistently use that could be holding you back? What could you change?

Here are some examples:

I can't —> I think I can

I have to —> I get to

I hate —> I prefer something else

You are not your thoughts. The more you can take a step back and step into the observer role, the more you can become consciously aware of the thoughts you think, the words you use and the control they have over your experiences.

Your thoughts, words and beliefs pack a lot of energy. They are what fuels your engine. Isn't it time to make sure that the energy you are putting out into the world, and using to fuel the direction of your life, is working in your favor?

I often hear women ask, "When should I be ready to move on?" or "When should I be over him?" There are a couple things that stand out to me with these questions. First, there is no expected timeline. Everyone has their own process of healing and moving forward, and no one can determine what might be right or best for you.

The second thing that stands out is the word "should." Using this word can set you up for unrealistic expectations and lead to feelings of fear, panic, and shame. In this sense, "should" is considered an unhealthy cognitive distortion, otherwise considered an internal filter that makes you feel worse about yourself. These irrational or distorted beliefs and thought patterns can be detrimental to our overall health, confidence, success, and more.

There are a variety of these cognitive distortions. Below, I have included some examples.

- Black and white thinking/ All-or-Nothing Thinking - "I always end up with the worst men."
- Mind reading/Jumping to Conclusions: "My partner is going to leave me (when there is no evidence of this)."
- Personalization- "It is all my fault."
- Overgeneralization - "There are no good men."
- Comparison- "I will never be able to have a life like hers."
- Catastrophizing- "No one will love me. I am going to be alone forever."
- Disqualifying the positive- "Nobody cares about me (despite having three quality friends who care very much)."
- Labeling- "I am broken."

"When you know better, you do better." – Maya Angelou

So now that we know what cognitive distortions are, how do we work to change our beliefs and thought patterns? I work through a process of reframing and rephrasing with my clients. The process looks something like this:

1. Awareness- the more you are aware of the beliefs you have or your typical way of thinking, the more you can seek to change the negative patterns. How often do you think negatively? If you tend to lean negatively most of the time, you may tend to have a negative bias.

Notice when you tend to think more negatively? Is there something that triggers these emotions or thought patterns?

2. Test the evidence- Are these thoughts true? What is the evidence to support my thinking? Sometimes simply identifying a lack of supporting evidence can help diffuse the negative thought or emotion. If it still feels intense or you are unsure if it is real, ask yourself if there is possibly another reason or perspective you haven't considered.

3. Journaling- As with any desire to change, journaling can be very beneficial. You can journal about your thoughts, when they occurred, what prompted them, and how you felt. As you write these occurrences down, you may begin to notice patterns. Additionally, when you are beyond the negative energy of the moment, you can consider alternate thoughts that may have a more positive perspective. Once you have created some positive alternatives, you can begin to implement these shifts as you are struggling with the negative thinking or distortions.

4. De-catastrophizing- If you are stuck in catastrophic thinking, try asking, "What is the worst-case scenario?" Get as detailed as possible. As you begin to walk through the worst-case scenario, you will begin to identify the likelihood of that situation as well as an increased awareness that you would be able to handle it. This technique is particularly helpful for those who suffer from anxiety or panic attacks in certain situations.

5. Reframe, Replace, Rephrase- when you notice yourself thinking negatively, immediately ask yourself: how can I reframe this thought? What positive thought can I replace this negative thought with? How can I rephrase this way of thinking? These shifts may be challenging at first but the more you do them the more automatic they will become. Over time you will likely notice your negative thinking decreasing and your positive thinking or reframing increase.

WINK

Shifting your mindset takes practice, particularly because you were most likely conditioned from a very early age. We tend to adopt similar mindsets and thought patterns to those around us, including our parents or caregivers. Mindfulness and shifting your thought patterns are a practice and require both time and effort.

The first mindset practice that I started was a gratitude practice. While at one of the safe houses, I committed to naming three things I was grateful for ever day before I climbed out of bed. I encourage you to adopt a similar practice, whenever it works best for you- when you wake up, while you are in the shower or before you go to sleep at night. Name 3-5 things you are grateful for in your life, or specifically referencing that day. One piece of advice, many people focus on the material things, but I challenge you to (also) think about people, experiences, pets, etc.

Activity

I recommend choosing one area to focus on if you are in a place where you want to change your thought patterns. Trying to do too much at once will become overwhelming, and you will likely not follow through with any of them. Pick one and try to be consistent with it. I like to set a goal of 2-4 weeks when starting out with something new. If you notice yourself falling "off the wagon" get back on and try to be proactive longer than you were on your last attempt. Change takes time and it is important to be patient with yourself.

Chapter 18
Out-of-the-Box Healing

Photography

9/11/19

If only I could see myself the way you capture me through your lens

I know it sounds strange but several months ago it dawned on me that I almost never look at my face when I'm in front of a mirror. I acknowledge several emotions that came up for me. Fear, not feeling good enough, not feeling pretty enough, shame and embarrassment. Afraid of what I might see. Ashamed of the woman staring back at me. Ashamed to see a woman who had been beaten down for so long. A woman who felt so unworthy that she tolerated being torn apart day after day. One day, though, something changed. No, she didn't begin to see herself in the mirror but rather she saw herself in a photograph and she was proud. She saw a reflection she didn't recognize. She saw a woman she wanted to become. She saw power, strength and beauty unlike any she had recognized before. So, when you want to accuse me of being self-absorbed and obsessed with my looks, please understand maybe I am in a way, but in this space in front of a camera, I am gaining more knowledge of who I am and who I want to be. I am getting an intimate lesson about myself. I am learning that I am strong and powerful but also soft, beautiful and sexy. I am proud of the work I am able to create in that space.

I began to discover my confidence and began to see me for me through photos. It certainly is not a textbook modality for healing, but photoshoots became a tool in my toolbox that had a profound impact on my journey. I dipped my toe into photoshoots and modeling when I was competing in the fitness industry. I had been admiring a specific photographer for some time and desperately wanted to shoot with him. In the midst of my divorce, I was finally able to secure a session while I was home for the holidays.

I walked in blind to something I had never experienced before. I felt shy and somewhat uncomfortable bearing my naked body for others to paint in glitter. I was insecure in my body and in who I was. I trembled walking through the cold warehouse as I prepared to have all eyes on me. The more we worked together, the more I began to warm up and feel more comfortable in my skin, or should I say, the layer of glitter and sparkle?

Prior to leaving, the photographer thanked me for my trust in him and shared a couple of shots from the back of his camera. My breath caught in my chest. My immediate thought was, "how is it possible, how is that me?"

When I finally saw the finished product a few weeks later, I stared at them for hours. I didn't recognize the woman in those shots. She looked comfortable and confident. She looked strong and courageous. She looked so different from the way I felt.

Over the years, I did more photoshoots. I began to feel more sure of myself in front of the camera but I still remain in awe of the way the lens captures me. I always wonder how the camera can see me in a way that I never have.

I have leveraged this newfound confidence and used it in other areas of my life too. I learned that others may see me very differently than I see myself. I learned that maybe I see myself through a corrupt lens that was programmed when I was a child and never outgrew. I learned that I could adopt personas, embodying characteristics of a woman I would like to be rather than the girl I see myself as.

I learned that I could tell stories through my photos. I learned that this could be a safer way of sharing my truth without needing anyone to believe a word I said, because they could so easily connect to the emotions of the image.

Hiking Is My Happy Place

Hiking became my energy source after moving back to Colorado. When I was young, I didn't appreciate all this state had to offer. Now that I was back, I was in awe of its beauty.

My first year back I hiked every Saturday, if not more often. I was not a fan of the early mornings but when I pulled into the parking lot at the trailhead, I was ready to go. I loved everything about it from the cool, crisp morning air to the smell of pine trees and dirt, to the bluebird skies.

I always had my phone in my hand, ready to document every flower, every beautiful sight that left me pinching myself. I also realized later that an effect of my trauma was difficulty with my memory. By capturing these photos on the mountain, I could look back in the days and weeks to come and recall the breathtaking hikes I was able to take. The photos also allowed me a second chance to experience the peace and calm that I felt out there, in simply bringing that memory forward.

Hiking, in nature, disconnected from the busyness of the world, allowed me to reconnect with myself. It allowed me the time and space to think and to gain clarity in the midst of chaos and confusion. It allowed me to feel safe in the quiet stillness that existed among the trees. Hiking was the place where I could finally take a deep breath and give a sigh of deep relief. In the mountains I felt free and I felt alive.

Being Present

Through meditation or other exercises, I have found a lot of comfort and power in the ability to be fully present. I have a friend who often says, "Be present where your feet are." Focusing on the present moment, whether in meditation, through breathwork, or some other intentional exercise, allows me to take my mind off the "What Ifs." Presence eases my anxiety and my fear. Presence allows me to experience a calm peacefulness, even if just for a few minutes. I have learned that meditative practices do not require a lot of time to have massive impacts. Even five minutes can help to ground you into the present moment and allow you to give your attention to the here and now.

Ridin' Solo

Lastly, I immersed myself in solo adventures. Some included meeting up with others, none of whom I knew, while other adventures afforded me some much-needed one-on-one time.

I wanted to become comfortable with myself because I truly believed the better I knew myself the less likely I would be to lose myself again in a relationship. I took myself on dates, out to dinner, to the movies and to the theater. I went to events, joined in on group trips and eventually traveled alone.

Having the opportunity to follow my heart and see the things on my bucket list has been game changing. I wasn't at the mercy of another person. I didn't have to argue with someone about where I wanted to go, what time to leave, how much time to spend or even what I spent my money on. Being fully in charge gave me a sense of confidence and accomplishment. It also allowed me to clearly think about what I wanted to do and why. Solo adventures allowed me to add so much more meaning in my life that I likely would never have considered had I stayed in my relationship or even jumped into another relationship shortly after my divorce.

There are a variety of healing modalities such as psychotherapy (talk therapy), psychotherapeutics (medication), eye movement reprocessing, somatic work, inner child work, shadow work, hypnosis, ayahuasca retreats and more. Some of these interventions have bodies of research to prove their efficacy, while others simply rely on anecdotal experiences. The truth is, we are each unique individuals and therefore, we will respond differently to different types of treatment. The downside of that is it may require a lot of trial and error to find what works for you. Above I identified some of the most impactful, and non-traditional, forms of healing for me.

WINK

I am a huge proponent for tried and true, evidence-based approaches for healing, particularly when it comes to trauma. And yet the greatest areas of my personal growth have come from standing in front of a camera lens, showing myself how brave I can be and exploring on my own accord. All that to say, everyone has their own process and their own unique tools that work for them. If you find something that works, I encourage you to embrace it and use it to support you in your own healing journey.

Activity

Consider some out-of-the-box healing strategies you could add to your toolbox. Do this by identifying three things for each of the following (they can repeat):

Where do I feel most peaceful?

1. _____

2. _____

3. _____

When do I feel most confident?

1. _____

2. _____

3. _____

With whom can I be my truest self?

1. _____

2. _____

3. _____

Where do I feel most free?

1. _____

2. _____

3. _____

When do I feel most alive?

1. _____

2. _____

3. _____

Are there any common themes? How can you begin to incorporate these strategies into your everyday life? (That could be on a daily, weekly or monthly basis.)

Chapter 19
E is for Embodiment

10/24/2017

The thought that keeps repeating itself in my head is, "he has released me."

You have released me from this cycle. You have released me from a relationship that was broken to its core. You have released me from the stress and worry about whether you were being faithful and honest. You have released me from wondering if I was the only one you loved. You have released me from wondering if you ever loved me. You have released me to live a life I deserve. You have released me to find a love that I deserve.

6/8/22

The year ahead is going to be something special; I can feel it. I'm making an impact in the space of women's healing work and creating ripples. I am financially compensated for the work I do because the world knows that it is how we can expand our reach as well as my ability to share my gifts. I'm speaking on the largest stage ever. I have a partner who adores me and respects me and values me.

What do I want love to feel like? I want it to feel like a breath of fresh air. I want love that feels like a deep sigh, a warm embrace. I want love to feel like coming home, a sense of easiness and the freedom to be exactly who I am at my core, in my most raw form, no masks, no facade and to be accepted for all of me. I want love to feel like excitement and passion; An eagerness for more but also calm, safe and peaceful.

I want love to feel like and to be an adventure exploring each other and exploring all the world wants to offer together. I want the sex to feel safe, love-filled, free to explore, passionate and orgasmic. I want love and my relationship to feel like a wild adventure and coming home all wrapped in one. I want long, beautiful, inspiring, invoking conversations. I want encouragement to pursue my passions. I want mutual adoration. I want us to do big things and be so proud of one another. I want respect, integrity, trust, excitement, pride, pure love, deep connection, and intimacy.

"If you inherently long for something, become it first. If you want gardens, become the gardener. If you want love, embody love. If you want mental stimulation, change the conversation. If you want peace, exude calmness. If you want to fill the world with artists, begin to paint. If you want to be valued, respect your own time. If you want to live ecstatically, find the ecstasy within yourself. This is how to draw it in, day by day, inch by inch." – Victoria Erickson

I had to start believing in myself. I had to start investing in me and my future.

One morning, while in bed at a safe house in the early days of my divorce, I woke to the sun coming in through the windows. Something in me had shifted. I recalled how miserable I thought my mom had become after her divorce. I didn't understand it at the time. But in that moment, I felt the anger, the rage and the resentment building inside me. I felt the bitterness boiling. I was furious about the lies. I was distraught about the infidelity. I was questioning everything. I realized how I could just as easily be affected. I realized that if I did not decide to change how I would perceive my experience in this moment, I would end up just like her. Before I pulled back the covers, I made the commitment to myself that I would not succumb to this. I would not let this divorce, this end of a relationship, this rejection, be the end of me.

That day I started a gratitude practice. I would list 3-5 things I was grateful for before getting out of bed each morning. It wasn't always easy, and some days it was a downright struggle, but I knew I needed to continue to focus on the good.

I also began to shift my perspective of the situation from one where I felt rejected and robbed to one where I was given an opportunity to recreate my life from this point forward. I thought that the divorce papers were my chance at a new life. I remember hearing a saying over and over in my head, "He released me." I was finally free to choose to do life on my terms. I was finally free to create a life that would make me happy. In that moment, I considered what I would or could do now that I was free.

I would travel to all the places on my bucket list and I would get a 50% discount because I would no longer need to pay for my husband. I would start a business where I could support women in similar situations. I would work with a coach to hold me accountable and help me set goals for my new future.

When I went after the things that I wanted, and believed they truly could happen for me, things began to change.

In preparation for writing this book, I scoured old journals, mostly dating back to 2017 but some as far back as 2003. Something that I had begun doing in 2018 was to write down exactly how I wanted my life to look and feel. At times I would write letters with generalizations, other times I would document a day-in-the-life of my future self or write letters to my future partner expressing my gratitude for our relationship.

Embodying the woman you are ready to become is a transformative and empowering process. It involves stepping into your authentic self, embracing your strengths, and embracing the possibilities of growth and self-actualization.

On this journey of self-reflection and self-discovery, you have begun to understand your values, passions, and desires. When you have a greater understanding of your true and authentic self, you can align your actions and choices with the woman you aspire to be.

You are letting go of past identities and limiting beliefs, including those negative narratives you may have internalized as a result of your experiences. Embodying this new version of you will require you to fully shed these limiting beliefs, recognize your inherent worthiness, and reframe your self-perception with self-compassion and love.

The greater clarity you have around the woman you aspire to be and all she embodies, the clearer you will be about the steps necessary to become her. This process will empower you to take charge of your life, embrace your potential, and cultivate a sense of purpose and fulfillment.

Building a network of like-minded individuals who share similar aspirations and values creates an environment that nurtures growth and accountability. Connecting with others who have gone through similar journeys can provide inspiration, guidance, and validation along the path of personal transformation.

This stage of embodiment is the culmination of all the work you have done to this point. You are clear on who you are and what you want. You know your value, and you have a better sense of self-esteem and self-worth. You are stepping into your authenticity and creating boundaries that protect the woman you have become. Embodying this woman is nothing new, it is simply refining and continuing to integrate the self-discovery work you have been doing and continue to do.

When you close your eyes and imagine the woman you want to be, your brain has trouble differentiating between reality and the visualization. For that reason, it is important to get clear on as many details as you can. What do you see? What environment are you in? Who is with you? What do you feel, both in your body and the tactile sensations around you? What smells are there? For some, this can be a challenging detail because we get caught up in the silliness of it. However, some smells I have used in the past would be coffee brewing to greet me in the morning. Or the smell of the pine trees as I step out onto my deck. What are you doing? Are you working, or gardening or are you curled up in a chair writing in your journal as you drink your hot coffee?

The reason this exercise is important is because one of our biggest limitations to growth is that we don't believe we can achieve what we want, we don't believe that it is possible, or we don't believe that it is possible for us. The more you can visualize and feel into this experience, the more you allow your brain to believe that this is your reality which helps to minimize the challenges that would have otherwise gotten in your way.

Also, some think this feels a little too woo woo, but I want to remind you that athletes use the power of visualization all the time. When I was younger and competing in both gymnastics and cheerleading, my coaches would repeatedly have us visualize a perfect routine before going out on the floor. College and Olympic athletes report doing this as well. They visualize a perfect game, the perfect catch, the perfect kick, and so on. You not only need to have the physical skills to make it possible, but you also need to have the belief that it is possible for you.

The second exercise that I find incredibly valuable for this idea of embodiment is to identify areas of your life where you already embody this woman. For example, one characteristic of the woman I wanted to embody was confidence in who she was and what she was capable of. I thought about areas of my life where I feel like I have that confidence. I know that when I walk into a gym, particularly one that I am familiar with, I feel unstoppable. I have the confidence in myself, that I am meant to be there and that I am capable of doing the hard things. While in a therapy session, my therapist encouraged me to feel that same level of confidence the next time I walked into a coffee shop.

I love this exercise because you already have the skills necessary, once again you need to just believe in yourself. In therapy we call this generalizing. If you're like me, you can walk confidently in a gym but now you need to prove to yourself that you can walk just as confidently out on the sidewalk. It is no different in terms of the foundation, the only difference is overcoming your lack of belief in yourself.

How can you show up today as the woman you want to be?

- How does she feel in her body?
- How does she dress?
- How does she approach others?
- How do others approach her?
- What does she think of herself?
- What do others think of her?
- How does she command her stage?
- Does she call the shots?
- What lifestyle does she live?
- What does her life look like?

WINK

Embodying the woman you want to become may feel uncomfortable at first. In many ways it requires a mental shift, but it also creates an energetic shift within you. You are more confident, you are more open to opportunities, you are more approachable. You never know how these minor changes could potentially alter your entire trajectory.

Activity

Visualization

Take a few minutes to spend some time to yourself for the following visualization. Find a comfortable space to sit or lie down, with as little distraction as possible. Make sure you can relax into this moment and close your eyes, if that feels safe.

Think of someone you believe is thriving. What does their life look like? What do they do regularly? Who do they surround themselves with? What are they wearing? Where do they spend most of their time? How do you think they feel? Once you have explored as many little details as you can imagine, I want you to now visualize that it is you. You are the one who is thriving.

What does your life look like? What are you doing regularly? Or what does your day-to-day look like? Where are you living? Who are you surrounded by? Where are you spending most of your time? Are you married? Do you have kids? Are you working? What are you wearing? What is important to you? How do you feel?

Allow yourself to really feel into this visualization. Stay here, soaking it all in, as long as it feels comfortable.

If you are someone who likes to journal, I encourage you to write down these details so you can come back to it often. Believing that this is a possibility for you is what will truly make it so.

I have some clients who do this visualization activity as part of their daily routine. You can't visualize your future, and all that you want, too often.

Chapter 20
What Does It Mean to Thrive?

12/2019

Can I be accepting of where I am today?

I have overcome violence, trauma, emotional abuse, constant degradation and yet I choose to be optimistic about where I am in life and what I have control over. I have learned that I am stronger and more powerful than I ever would have imagined. I can handle being on my own. I have come to learn how easy it is for me to navigate my own way and enjoy my own company. No matter how much we try to take control and take the lead, though, the universe may have other plans. We can tighten our grip and do everything in our power to try to see the direction in which we think our life should go, only to realize there are times when we have to let go and trust that what is coming is far better than what we have.

"I have come to the conclusion that human beings are born with an innate capacity to triumph over trauma. I believe not only that trauma is curable, but that the healing process can be a catalyst for a profound awakening – a portal opening to emotional and genuine spiritual transformation." – Peter A. Levine

Healing is not easy, and healing is not linear. I frequently think of healing on a continuum that overlays Maslow's Hierarchy of Needs. I believe you must ensure that your basic needs, including a sense of security and protection, are met before you can truly begin the journey of healing. If your body is consistently in survival mode, you cannot relax enough to begin to heal or grow.

If we look at Maslow's Hierarchy it starts with physiological needs, then safety and security, followed by love and belonging, then self-esteem and finally self-actualization. Similarly, what I have dubbed The Healing Hierarchy, follows the trajectory from safety and security to doing the healing work, to growth, followed by sovereignty, and then, the ultimate goal of thriving. Let me be clear, though, while I think a hierarchy is a nice visual, by no means do I truly believe our healing follows this type of pattern. Sometimes you may jump around or feel as though you have gone backwards. It is important to know that there is no predicted path or right way to heal.

Maslow's Hierarchy of Needs   The Healing Hierarchy

Beyond the healing work, beyond simply surviving, however, is thriving. If you know that there is no "end zone" or finality to the healing journey, what would success look like for you? How would you define thriving in your own life?

I used to be that girl that thought success would mean that I was thriving. I thought it meant that If I landed a great job, a really good salary, got married, bought a house, checked all the boxes, I would be thriving. Because of my upbringing and my limiting beliefs, my idea of thriving was based on the need for external validation, love and praise.

Through my healing journey, described in this book, I learned how far off track I was. Thriving isn't about checking the boxes. In reality, for me, thriving is about feeling fulfilled, feeling a sense of peace and calm, feeling grateful for each day, and having a deep connection with the people I have in my life.

On my podcast, Rise Up Thriving, I interview women who have overcome adversity and found their own ability to thrive, despite their circumstances. At the end of several interviews, I asked these women what it means to thrive. Here are some of their responses:

"Thriving is feeling free to be myself; to be who and what I am. And to be engaged with every area of my life." – Kristi Chaves

"Thriving means to be in a fulfilled place; coming back to what really lights you up. Living from a passionate place where you are able to step into your fullest truth by being in your joy." – Maria Altamirano

"Thriving is bringing the magic and meaning into every day." – Francesca Brundsen

"Thriving is, simply, to be happy." – Dayle Sheehan

At the end of the day, thriving is however you choose to define it. Similar to the Life Audit exercise at the beginning of the book, I like to give a Thriving exercise as well, called THRIVEMAPP. This "Map" of sorts can help give you clarity on the things that are supporting or detracting from your ability to thrive.

I believe, like the journey in the book, the ability to thrive is made up of the following:

(T) Thoughts- What is your state of mind, particularly knowing now how much your mindset influences your life?

(H) Habits and Patterns- What habits and patterns are serving you and what may need to be changed (in order for you to truly thrive)?

(R) Relationships- What is the quality of the primary relationships in your life? Are they enhancing your life or taking away from your potential?

(I) Identity- Who do you identify as? Do you identify as a person who is thriving? If not, what needs to shift?

(V) Values- Are you living in accordance with your values? Do you know what your core values are? Are your day-to-day actions aligned with your core values?

(E) Experiences- Are you engaging in experiences that are making your life better or making your life worse? What experiences would someone who is thriving engage in?

(M) Meaning- What is your reason for living? What gives your life meaning?

(A) Accountability- Do you have anyone holding you accountable to living your fullest life? Who is counting on you to show up? Who needs you to be your best self?

(PP) Purposeful Productivity- You can be busy, but does your busyness have purpose? In fact, evidence shows that when your day-to-day tasks have a greater purpose, you will in turn have more life satisfaction, as well as improved mental health and wellbeing.

When we take time to recognize how interconnected it all is, we can begin to see the bigger picture. We can understand the cascading effects of our thoughts, actions and meaning making.

Are you someone who continues to define success by what was once known as the "American Dream," or can you unsubscribe from that conditioned thinking and create your own definition of thriving?

WINK

What if someone offered you a magic pill that allowed you to have the life you truly desire? Unfortunately, there is no magic pill. However, when you commit to doing the work, you realize that the life of your dreams is within your grasp. It won't come easy, and it will take time, but it is possible.

Activity

Conduct your own Thrive Audit. You can find the instructions for the THRIVEMAPP process at www.risewithkristina.com/book1

Conclusion

Steve Jobs once said, "You can't connect the dots looking forward; you can only connect them looking backwards. So, you have to trust that the dots will somehow connect in your future."

You may not have recognized the toxicity, or the trauma caused, while you were in the midst of it. You were just merely trying to survive. But there's a reason you picked up this book. You know there is something more for you in your future. You know that you didn't go through what you did for nothing. But in order to get there, you must first do the work required to heal. Healing is necessary because the wounds that are left unhealed will continue to trap you in a past that you are desperate to break free from, even if you are not consciously aware of it yet.

As I have shared in the previous pages, my own experience has been anything but easy. I have uncovered wounds that I never would have realized were simmering just beneath the surface, without this one catalyst. Those early moments of inquiry may be the very thing that will lead you down a path you never expected. Use the R.I.S.E. Method so that you too can triumph after trauma. Take the time to (R)ecognize when things don't feel right. Do the (I)nformation Gathering and research so you are well equipped to make the right decisions for you. Go through the (S)elf-Discovery process so that you can take life back into your own hands. And begin to (E)mbody the woman that you were always meant to be.

My friend Telma says, "Life is gonna life." The point of doing the work is not to make sure nothing challenging ever comes your way again. The fact remains that there will be more hardship, more adversity, and there may even be more rock bottoms. However, with the right tools and resources, hopefully you can keep yourself from falling so far down or staying there as long because now you are capable of picking yourself back up.

What started with initial questions around my happiness led to a total disruption of my life as I knew it. There was so much pain and heartache but to be on the other side, I can adamantly declare that I am so glad I was willing to go through it all.

Despite the questions of how I could stay as long as I did, or why was I willing to put up with such horrible behavior, I can now accept that I didn't know any better. I was under the spell of manipulation; I had low self-esteem and didn't have healthy relationship models I could look to. I also didn't have adults in my life in whom I could confide.

Though the decision to break free literally led me to fear for my life for years after, I am so grateful that I have broken the cycle. I am now in a loving, respectful, and healthy relationship. I now have other relationships I can look to and a support system that is there for me.

And that is my wish for you. I want you to experience the deep sigh that comes when you can finally stop "just surviving." The relief that comes from knowing that you are learning how to break cycles and doing the work to heal old wounds.

The knowledge that when we heal together, we rise together. When you do your healing work, you create ripples that affect everyone you meet. While that may sound extreme, consider how much your mood affects your energy, your conversations, your generosity, your willingness to do for others, the smile you have on your face, and so on. The simple act of smiling and being kind to someone often results in the same behavior from them for another and so on. This is what the ripples are all about.

I also hope, through my story, you have been able to recognize there is no right way to heal and no one way to heal. We are each unique in our experiences, how we learn, how we process and what feels best. I encourage you to experiment. Take time to explore who you are, take time to explore what feels good, and take time to honor your needs.

You deserve to feel great, optimistic and in love with your life. You deserve to have love, deep friendships, and a dependable support system.

And last but not least, I want you to know that you are enough just as you are, and you matter. The world needs you.

WINK

So many of my journal entries documented the chaos and confusion I felt in my own healing journey. We want it to be linear and to make sense. We want it to move quickly and easily. And yet, now that I am so much further along in the process, I see why things had to happen the way they did and why I needed the lessons I learned. Even if you feel like a pinball in a pinball machine, that is normal. It won't last forever and one day you will look back from a place of calm contentment.

If you need additional support, I highly recommend working with a trauma-informed therapist or a coach. Therapists vary in their approaches as well as their expertise, as do coaches. Do your due diligence to research the best approach for you. A word of caution would be to avoid those who promise quick fixes or a full recovery. Healing takes years and rather than thinking of it as an end zone, think of it as a new level of awareness. Healing isn't allowing you to get over something, but rather it allows you to move through.

Activity

You can find a list of my favorite books and resources at www.risewithkristina.com/book1

References

1. U.S. Department of Health & Human Services, Administration for Children and Families, Administration on Children, Youth and Families, Children's Bureau. (2021). Child Maltreatment 2019. Available from https://www.acf.hhs.gov/cb/research-data-technology/ statistics-research/child-maltreatment.

2. Hunter, Cathryn. "Effects of Child Abuse and Neglect on Adult Survivors. Australian Institute of Family Studies." Aifs.gove.au, Jan. 2014. https://aifs.gov.au/resources/policy-and-practice-papers/effects-child-abuse-and-neglect-adult-survivors

3. Egeland, B., Jacobvitz, D., & Sroufe, L. A. (1988). Breaking the Cycle of Abuse. *Child Development*, *59*(4), 1080–1088. https://doi.org/10.2307/1130274

4. Jaffee SR, Bowes L, Ouellet-Morin I, Fisher HL, Moffitt TE, Merrick MT, Arseneault L. Safe, stable, nurturing relationships break the intergenerational cycle of abuse: a prospective nationally representative cohort of children in the United Kingdom. J Adolesc Health. 2013 Oct;53(4 Suppl):S4-10. doi: 10.1016/j.jadohealth.2013.04.007. PMID: 24059939; PMCID: PMC4212819.

Next Steps

Thank you so much for taking the time to read my first book, Rise Up & Thrive. Though I pulled from my own past experiences, the goal is really to support you in your own journey of healing and growth.

I would love to connect with you and support you. You can find me at www.risewithkristina.com and to access the resources identified throughout the book, go to www.risewithkristina.com/book1

Acknowledgments

This book would not have been possible without the endless love and support from so many people in my life.

Less than six months before my grandmother passed, unexpectedly, she asked me when I was going to write a book. The idea had been swirling around in my head for many years at that point, but I still hadn't made the commitment to bring it to life. A few short months later, I signed up with my book writing coach, Jake Kelfer, to finally make the dream a possibility.

I won't be able to thank everyone who stood by my side and cheered me on throughout the process, but I do want to make sure to acknowledge some people who truly breathed belief into me day in and day out.

The woman who started as an acquaintance and accountability partner, turned incredible friend and confidant, I would not be here without you, Telma Sanchez.

JZ, for loving me and supporting me throughout this process. From the flowers and messages of encouragement, you kept reminding me of what was possible and what so many other women needed to hear. Thank you for showing me what a healthy, loving relationship can look and feel like.

My sister, Kerri, who is my best friend through thick and thin. Thank you for always showing up for me, particularly when I felt as though my world was falling apart.

My guardian angel, Denae Zoellner, who came into my life at exactly the right time. Thank you for shining your light and bringing so much love, laughter and joy into my life.

My cousins, Brad and Mandy, for loving and supporting me. You helped me pick up the pieces (literally) and helped me to build myself back to the woman I am today.

Brett Seeley, an incredibly talented photographer, who not only helped me see a different side of myself but also encouraged me to grow in ways I didn't think were possible.

Thank you, Carol King, for your friendship and for creating a safe container where you posed questions that have contributed to my deepest healing.

Candace Pearson, thank you for your friendship and support over these last six years of my greatest challenges and greatest growth.

My deepest gratitude to my many mentors and therapists over the years. I have been taught that my greatest mirrors come from my relationships, and I would not be where I am without these reflections from which I continue to heal and grow.

I extend my appreciation to anyone I may have forgotten. There are too many individuals to name but your impact does not go unnoticed.

My Ask, Please Share A Review!

I have one last request for you!

If you have enjoyed this book and the resources provided,
I would be thrilled if you took a few minutes to write a review wherever
you bought this book.
So many women are struggling to get out of and heal from toxic
relationships. Without these strategies, women may never have the
opportunity to thrive. If you feel called to share your honest feedback, you
may help get this message in the hands of the women who need it most.

Author Bio

 Kristina Hudson helps women break cycles of toxic and traumatic relationships so that they can cultivate healthy love that lasts. She is the founder and host of the Rise Up Thriving Podcast, as well as a speaker and coach.

Kristina went from being an occupational therapist specializing in military-related brain injuries and post-traumatic stress disorder to helping women discover their resilience and confidence after trauma. She felt called to work specifically with women who have experienced toxicity and trauma in relationships after her own fight to not only survive, but to thrive.

Made in the USA
Monee, IL
28 June 2024

60879095R00085